ACROSS A DEADLY FIELD

THE WAR IN THE EAST

JOHN HILL

COVER ARTIST: MARK STACEY

OSPREY
PUBLISHING

First published in Great Britain in 2014 by Osprey Publishing,
PO Box 883, Oxford, OX1 9PL, UK
 PO Box 3985, New York, NY 10185-3985, USA
E-mail: info@ospreypublishing.com

Osprey Publishing is part of the Osprey Group

Print ISBN: 978 1 4728 0261 3
PDF e-book ISBN: 978 1 4728 0262 0
EPUB e-book ISBN: 978 1 4728 0263 7

Typeset in Berling and Rosewood
Maps by Todd Davis

Originated by PDQ Media, Bungay, UK
Printed in China through Worldprint Ltd.

14 15 16 17 18   10 9 8 7 6 5 4 3 2 1

www.ospreypublishing.com

Osprey Publishing is supporting the Woodland Trust, the UK's leading woodland
conservation charity, by funding the dedication of trees.

CONTENTS

ACKNOWLEDGEMENTS

As was the case with the *Across a Deadly Field* wargame rules, this book and its scenarios could not have been developed, play-tested and refined without the help of many others. First among many would be my wife, Luella – a true wargame widow – who not only put up with my obsession with the battles of yesteryear, but contributed by meticulously and tediously calculating all the "point values" for all the units that were at – or could have been at – the first day of Gettysburg. For you guys that like to create point-based civil war armies, thank her, not me.

As I have said many times, no one can create this stuff by themselves. It takes the insights and hard work of many talented and dedicated individuals. Dean West with his encyclopaedic knowledge of the horse and musket period was relentless in his determination that every little historical detail and nuance was correctly portrayed. His fanatical devotion to historical accuracy clearly shows in the two 1864 Shenandoah Valley scenarios he created for this book. But history is more than a myriad of tactical details. It is "flavor" and "feel," and Duke Seifried – the grandmaster of miniature gaming – was equally persistent in his constant insistence that while detail is good, it must never overshadow the "flow, the flavor and the feel" of the game, as that is what makes a game fun. If it isn't fun, then it won't be played and if it isn't played, then it isn't a game – point taken.

Patrick LeBeau, John Hill and Dean West present The First Day of Gettysburg at Nashcon 2014. (Chris Ward)

ADF and its scenarios are not just history, it is a game, and a game requires rules that have to clearly convey the designers' intent in a manner that allows the gamers to "creatively" use all the historically correct tactics of the period while at the same time reining in the use of historically inappropriate game mechanics. Those people that can understand the designer's intent and can burrow into the written rules to make sure that everything that is good is preserved and everything that is bad is kicked out are a rare breed indeed. They are the "rule makers and rule breakers." I was most fortunate to have the talents of four of the best – P. J. O'Neill, Patrick LeBeau, Todd Davis and Cory Ring. These guys would toil through every play test version of the rules, every movement and combat chart, and multiple rewrites of all of that, to make sure that the "how to play" was crystal clear in a manner that even the most diabolical of "rule lawyers" could not pervert. Then, to make sure the game worked as it should, they would present and run demo games at some of the major conventions. If there are any "legal loopholes" left, it is not their fault but mine, as I would inevitably do one more rewrite and inadvertently undo the rule thoroughness that they worked hard to put into the game.

But good miniature rules are much more than a thoroughly proofread and cross-referenced listing of "what to do" and "what not to do." All that has to be there, but they must also convey a sense of "visual spectacle." The rule book has to reflect the color, the drama and the "wow" factor that makes historical miniature wargaming so much more than just good history. And to do that you need expert graphics, which includes everything from clear diagrams of play to easy-to-read scenario maps and perfect tabletop photography. Those visual elements are what makes you want to pick up the paintbrush and crank out another regiment. Game graphics are no easy task – it is hard and incredibly time intensive, requiring a wide set of both artistic and technical skills. So, as you thumb through this book and become inspired by the graphics and pictures, thank Todd Davis, P. J. O'Neill, Patrick LeBeau and Dean West along with Alan Sheward, Chris Ward, Doug Kline, Malcom Johnston, Scott Mingus, and Cory Ring – who also deserves a special thanks for his extensive pre-release promotion of the ADF rules and scenarios on his *Cigar Box Battles* website.

Finally, I have to salute the most under-appreciated group of contributors to this and any wargame – the long suffering playtesters. These are the guys that willingly sign up to play a game that they know – at this stage – is almost certainly half-baked and that the rules will probably change in mid-game. Often, in terms of fun, it would be like volunteering to be the first "over the top" at the Somme. These are the true *grognards* who will go down whatever path the wargame designer sets for them. And I sincerely apologize if I cannot remember all of them – but some of those that were willing to do this again and again were Eric West, George Miksad, Stephen Geisinger, Justin Crouthamel, Kermit Hilles, Norris Darrall, Grant Daniels, Robert Hoy and Dana Lombardy. To any others I may have missed, my heartfelt thanks and appreciation.

John Hill

AN INTRODUCTION TO THE EASTERN SCENARIOS

FOR THE CONFEDERACY TO WIN THE WAR…

For the Confederacy to win the war it had to do more than fight defensive battles, as winning those only prolonged the war and a long war inevitably would be a war of attrition, which was a war the South could not win. Robert E. Lee saw that as clearly as did Ulysses S. Grant. After Lee's greatest victory of maneuver, the Battle of Chancellorsville, the South rejoiced – but Lee's emotions were much more measured. A larger host had indeed been forced to retreat in confusion, but the actual dead and wounded from the battle was just about the same for both sides – somewhat more than 10,000 for each – and the Virginia countryside continued to became even more depleted. To Lee, it was becoming clear that to

The charge of the 4th Texas at Gaine's Mill, June 27, 1861, by Stephen Walsh © Osprey Publishing Ltd. Taken from Campaign 133: Seven Days Battles 1862.

The Confederates mass their guns on Herr Ridge and Oak Hill in preparation for a coordinated assault. (Patrick LeBeau & Chris Ward)

win the Confederacy would have to break the Union's resolve to continue the war, as only that would undermine the political power base of the Lincoln administration. Then, and perhaps only then, would the North be willing to consider and possibly accept the division of the country. The South could and did win some impressive victories in the West – such as Chickamauga, which left a Union Army routed and besieged in Chattanooga – but such victories were not on the doorstep of Washington and consequently did not produce the required political shock effect. At Chattanooga, the Union merely brought in a different general – Ulysses S. Grant – and provided the resources to lift the siege. For the Union, it was business as usual.

For the South to win and to force the Union to accept a political separation would require the humbling of the North's premier military force, the Army of the Potomac, in a manner and location that would produce a political shockwave in Washington sufficient to fracture the administration's congressional support to continue the war. For the Confederacy, this created the conundrum that while the North could eventually win the war by winning in the West, the South could only win it by winning in the East, and winning it in a manner that would be perceived as threatening Washington itself. This fact was not lost on President Lincoln and was a major factor in his almost paranoiac insistence that the first mission of the Army of the Potomac must always be that of shielding Washington from any possible Confederate threat. While Lincoln's fixation on protecting Washington frequently made questionable military sense and resulted in a number of embarrassing setbacks, it did make perfect political sense, as Lincoln, perhaps more than some of his generals, instinctively knew what was at stake.

In an attempt to create the situation that could lead to a victory with political impact, General Robert E. Lee would directly threaten Washington or other significant northern cities three times: in 1862 with the Antietam campaign, in 1863 with the invasion of Pennsylvania and in 1864 when Lee sent Jubal Early north through the Shenandoah Valley. Each time, the Army of the Potomac responded to Lincoln's exhortations to place sufficient troops between the Confederates and Washington so as to block any threat. In 1862 and 1863, while Lee was successful in forcing the Army of the Potomac to redeploy and protect Washington, the major battles that did result – Antietam and Gettysburg – were hardly the decisive victory Lee was hoping for. And while Jubal Early's drive in 1864 did create some panic in the city, his 15,000 men were eventually checked by the Washington fortifications and the dispatch of three veteran divisions of the VI Corps from the Army of the Potomac. After the Union brought in even more troops, along with Major General Phil Sheridan, that was the end of any more threats from the Shenandoah Valley.

Of those three "invasions" the Gettysburg campaign was the most promising for Confederate hopes for a military victory that could translate into a political victory. The 1863 invasion came right on the heels of the Battle of Chancellorsville – yet another Union defeat in the East – and quickly drove through Maryland. Within weeks Confederates were in a position to threaten Harrisburg, the capital of Pennsylvania. Unlike the 1862 invasion that culminated with the Confederates quickly going on the defensive around Antietam creek, this time it appeared to many in Washington that the rebels had free reign throughout southern Pennsylvania and a choice as to which northern city they would sack first. The truth, of course, was much more nuanced and complex – but wars are often decided not by reality, but by perception. On July 1, 1863 outside of Gettysburg the Confederates had the opportunity to turn that perception into reality. Historically, that did not happen. However, throughout that day and the days preceding and following it decisions were made, not made, or changed by both sides that shaped the battle. Given the potential impact of those days of decisions – both large and small – on the course of the battle and possibly the war, this scenario book

dissects the First Day of Gettysburg using ten scenarios or scenario combinations reflecting both how it actually did and how it could have played out. In addition, a mini-campaign structure is included that can be used to play out one possible outcome of General George Meade's initially preferred option of fighting along Pipe Creek. This first scenario set of ten different Gettysburg scenarios that can be played individually or joined together will enable the wargamer or amateur historian to explore many of the "what ifs" or "should have dones" of the First Day of Gettysburg in a playable wargame format.

FOR THE UNION TO WIN THE WAR...

The battles and campaigns of the American Civil War were fought across the entire scope of the United States and its western territories. There was not an area that was untouched and almost every battle would have a local, regional and national impact. That said, some battles had greater impact than others and some theaters were more politically important than others. It has been argued that for the North to win they had to win first in the West, starting with the opening of the Mississippi and then slice through the heart of the Confederacy from Nashville to Atlanta. Then with its transportation, industrial and agricultural sectors destroyed, occupied or broken up, the effectiveness of the Southern armies would inexorably decline and the Confederacy would inevitably implode. The erosion of the South's military capacity would be accelerated by constantly opening new fronts, which in turn would stretch Richmond's dwindling economic and military resources ever thinner. In essence, that was the core of Lieutenant General Ulysses S. Grant's overall strategic plan for 1864 – "attack everywhere."

As long as the Union maintained the collective political will to continuously rebuild and expand its armies and to keep sifting through its generals until it found those that could win, while always looking for operations that could add another crisis requiring the Confederacy to find more troops to send to yet another front, then the North would prevail – if not this year, then perhaps the next. In this long view, the value of the Union's peripheral campaigns becomes more obvious as each one represents yet another emergency that would further divert critical Southern resources, so that at some point there would be one too many holes in the southern dike. In that context, this scenario book will examine battles from two frequently overlooked campaigns which on the surface appeared to accomplish little, but in reality were very much a part of Grant's grand strategy of "attack everywhere" and

The 20th Maine's stand on Little Round Top, by Adam Hook © Osprey Publishing Ltd. Taken from Campaign 52: Gettysburg 1863.

contributed in no small measure to the overextension of Lee's army, which would finally lead to its surrender.

One was the Shenandoah Campaign in the late spring of 1864, which started with a Union Army under Franz Sigel marching south through the Shenandoah Valley – the agricultural breadbasket of the Army of Northern Virginia – that immediately prompted General Breckenridge to respond with 4,000 soldiers. Though Sigel's force was soundly defeated at New Market, Breckinridge was promptly called east to assist Lee in countering Grant's continuous southward movement towards Cold Harbor. Meanwhile, within two weeks, a revitalized Union Army of the Shenandoah now under the aggressive General David Hunter again rolled southward through the Valley, and after defeating a sizable Confederate force at Piedmont advanced into Lynchburg, one of the major rail centers for western Virginia. This was a situation that had to be addressed, and Lee diverted Jubal Early with 14,000 men to drive Hunter out. Though it worked and Hunter fled into West Virginia, Lee now had that much less as he faced Grant's relentless assaults. Consequently, the two modest-sized battles of New Market and Piedmont would have a ripple effect beyond their local impact, and are the subject of two most elegant scenarios by one of this period's most noted wargame scholars, Dean West.

The second often overlooked campaign was launched in September of 1864 by Major General Ben Butler's Army of the James. Using a night march, Butler would take two corps across the James River and simultaneously launch two early morning attacks against two separate points of Richmond's outer defenses. Those outer defenses at New Market Heights and Fort Harrison were breeched as the Confederates had too few units to properly defend either. However, since continued Union success might have broken through to Richmond itself, Lee had to pull 8,000 men that could hardly be spared from the Petersburg front to contain and attempt to roll back this latest threat. Butler's offensive is represented by a scenario covering the attack on New Market Heights, which proved that the black soldiers of the United States Colored Troops (USCT) were the equal of any on the field. This little campaign, like the operations in the Shenandoah Valley in early 1864, constantly forced the Confederates to keep rotating fewer and fewer forces to more and more points of Union pressure. As Grant foresaw, it would be a process that, in time, could have only one inevitable result – Confederate military collapse and surrender.

ORGANIZATIONAL OPTIONS

USING GENERIC STANDS

For the historical gamer who likes his miniature regiments to have the correct regimental identification for the scenario he is playing, re-labeling all the stands for different scenarios could become quite tedious. Likewise, at different times, regiments would have vastly different strength. For instance, the 24th Michigan of the famed "Iron Brigade" started the Battle of Gettysburg on July 1 with over 480 men (8 figures), but by the end of the day had less than 240 men (4 figures), which would be its starting strength for any July 2 scenarios. So for the gamer that likes to have his regiments with the correct unit identification and approximate strength for the

specific battle he is simulating and is willing to have most of his soldiers painted as generic Union or Confederate soldiers, the following unit organizations tricks could prove useful.

For each regiment, paint up one small square stand with only one figure, a flag and a space for a unit ID. Then add generic stands to fill out the regiment for that particular battle. The one figure does not count for fire or melee but is there just for looks, so obviously an officer or drummer would be a good choice since they seldom fired anyway. The two Mississippi regiments shown in the diagram demonstrate this system in action, with the 11th Mississippi (Example 1) having 8 figures (480 men)

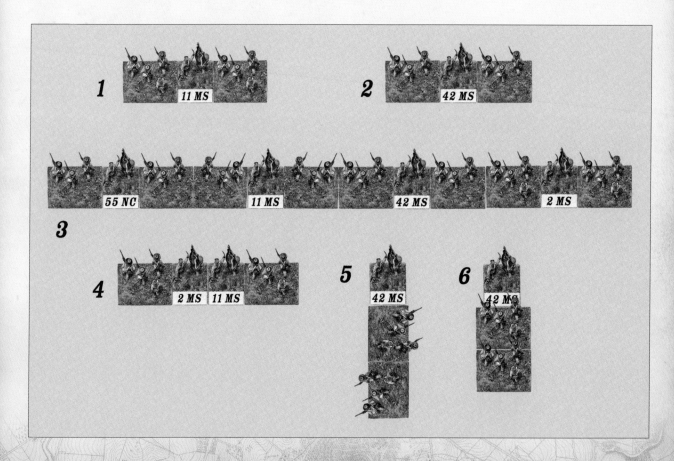

and the 42nd Mississippi (Example 2) having 6 figures (360 men).

Using this system makes it easy to see the individual regiments within a brigade line of many regiments (Example 3).

An advantage of this regimental marking system is that, it makes it easy to show a "merged" regiment that has been formed from two "depleted" one-stand regiments. Example 4 in the diagram shows a merged regiment formed from the depleted one-stand remnants of the 2nd Mississippi and the 11th Mississippi.

With only two stands per regiment, it can be difficult to distinguish between a road column and an attack column, particularly in terms of unit direction with the smaller figures. However, the use of a single flag stand also helps with that distinction. In Example 5, the 42nd Mississippi is in road column, while in Example 6 it is in attack column.

Finally, for those gamers who hate casualty markers *of any kind* on their units, using generic stands offers the option of tracking casualties by simply swapping out stands. If a unit with 8 figures (two 4-figure stands) loses a figure, simply replace one of the 4-figure stands with a 3-figure one, and if another figure is lost, replace that stand with a 2-figure stand.

TWO, THREE OR EVEN FOUR STANDS PER BRIGADE OR REGIMENT - THEY ALL WORK

The use of generic stands with different numbers of figures, when coupled with the fact that *Across a Deadly Field* works equally well with either 2- or 3-figure stands, offers the gamer the option of more precisely modeling the historical strength of both the very large and the very small units. For instance, the 16th Vermont at the start of Gettysburg would have a muster strength of almost 720 men, which could be modeled either with two stands of six figures each or three stands of four figures each. Likewise Lang's Brigade (a total of 740 men) of three small Florida regiments might best modeled as a single "unit" of two stands with six figures per stand, a 3-stand unit with four figures per stand, or even a 4-stand unit of three figures per stand, for a total of 12 figures. The only minor issue is that Basic Morale Point (BMP) degradation per stand is slightly different between a 2-stand unit, a 3-stand unit and a 4-stand unit, as so:

Unit Type	BMP 2-stand Units		BMP 3-stand Units			BMP 4-stand Units			
	2 stands	1 stand	3 stands	2 stands	1 stand	4 stands	3 stands	2 stands	1 stand
Green	6	12	6	9	12	6	8	10	12
Trained	5	10	5	7	10	5	6	8	10
Veteran	4	8	4	6	8	4	5	6	8
Elite	3	6	3	4	6	3	4	5	6

There is no reason why some regiments could not be portrayed as 2-stand regiments and others as 3-stand regiments – or even the rare enormous regiment of four stands – in the same battle, as long as it is noted which is which. That can easily be done by making a 3-inch by 5-inch brigade card with the characteristics of each regiment (its regiment identification, the number of stands, the number of figures, its weapons, its quality and its morale, and any special rules that apply to that particular regiment).

OPTIONAL RULES

The following additional rules can be applied to any *ADF* scenario and each highlights a particular tactical nuance of the civil war battlefield. While there is solid historical evidence for each of these rules, their use can add additional complexity or may alter play balance, and consequently they should be treated as rules that should be used only by mutual agreement between the players or by the game master's choice.

UNEQUAL STANDS

The basic rules for ADF have each regiment represented by two stands, each with the same number of figures, so that all units would be depleted at 50 percent casualties. However, for gamers that prefer to model specific regiments where the actual strength is known, a more accurate figure representation can be accommodated by not requiring that each stand have the same number of figures. For example, a 420-man regiment would be most accurately represented by a total of seven figures – one stand of four figures and one stand of three figures. If this is done, losses should be taken as follows:

If a regiment has unequal stands and it is an Elite or Veteran regiment, then losses are first taken on the stand with the most figures to show the greater resilience of these units. However, if that regiment is a Trained or Green regiment then its first losses should be taken against the stand with the least number of figures to show the greater fragility of less experienced units. Adapting this rule, however, tends to exaggerate the "staying power" of Elite and/or Veteran regiments versus Trained and/or Green regiments.

In ADF, regiments of two, three and even four stands can be used on the same gaming table. Here four large Union regiments are closing in on three Rebel regiments, two of which are obviously smaller units. (Alan Sheward)

The storming of Casey's Redoubt, by Steve Noon © Osprey Publishing Ltd. Taken from Campaign 124: Fair Oaks 1862.

VARIABLE ARRIVAL TIME

In any scenario where a specific arrival or entry time is indicated, that is the historical entry time as best as can be determined considering that even "reliable" historical sources often recorded significantly different times for the same events. There is always the possibility that an aggressive commander would have hurried his troops to the sound of the guns or, more likely, become a victim of unexpected traffic jams, confusion, or the always present frictions of war. To add those possibilities, use the following rule:

At the start of the scenario, roll a 1D6 for each arriving unit one turn before its scheduled arrival. If a 1 is rolled, then the unit comes in one turn earlier than scheduled – right now. If a 2, 3 or 4 is rolled, it comes in exactly as scheduled. If a 5 or 6 is rolled it comes in one turn later than originally scheduled. If there is a scheduled arrival sequence of brigades – such as Early's Confederate division – coming in at the same location, but sequenced one turn apart, roll once for the whole division to determine if the whole "sequence" is one turn early, on time, or delayed by one turn.

REGULAR DISENGAGEMENT

On a regular disengagement, the unit can stop running once it is behind friendly forces. However, on an "extreme disengagement" (see below) the unit must take the full disengagement movement distance. A disengaging unit drops one morale level, but never below "shaken".

EXTREME DISENGAGEMENT

The standard disengagement rule allows a unit to retreat with a double disorder move out of harm's way, with the firer losing one die and the retreating unit dropping one morale level. This rule assumes that the regimental commander is attempting to maintain some level of control of his regiment as they pull back. However, sometimes the situation has become so extreme that the disengagement becomes outright flight. Such was the case of Colonel Jesse Appler and the 53rd Ohio in the early hours of the Battle of Shiloh. After having repulsed two determined attacks by the 13th Tennessee, Appler suddenly lost his nerve and ordered "Retreat and save yourselves!" And run they did, with most of the regiment dissolving into a fleeing herd. To use this option, use the following rule.

If an infantry or cavalry unit wishes simply to run, it may make an "extreme disengagement." To do so, it retreats with a triple disorder move and all fire against it still loses one die. However, it ends its movement at two morale levels lower than when it began but never worse than routed. Hence a good-order unit will end as a shaken unit, but all others will end as a routed unit. As with a normal disengagement, an extreme disengagement can be done as an action or a reaction. If an artillery unit uses this option, it obviously would abandon its guns, so the battery would be removed.

ROAD COLUMN UNDER FIRE

Being in the wrong formation at the wrong time made even the best troops very nervous. One of the more unsettling conditions was being caught under fire while in a road column. By late 1862, even if a new politically-appointed brigade or division commander – or a new wargamer – did not know better, the regimental commanders and the soldiers themselves almost certainly did. To reflect their inherent battlefield awareness, incorporate this rule:

If a unit in road column comes under **any** fire that results in a morale check – regardless of whether the unit passes the morale check or not – that road column **must** immediately stop and use its next action or reaction to change formation into either a battle line or an extended line facing the enemy. If it was moving as part of its second action and consequently would not have an action left, it simply stops and **must** use its next reaction to change into a battle line or extended line.

CONTINUOUS MOVEMENT

The movement distances for ADF take into account the extra time it might take for the commanders to evaluate a situation, decide what they wanted to do, and have their orders clearly understood by their subordinates – all of which adds to operational delay. However, if all a regiment did was to move as fast as it could and that was clearly understood at the start of its "actions," and it did not stop to fire, reform and received no hostile fire during its continued movement, then it could go somewhat further than the "normal" distance for its two ADF actions. For example, on the first day of Gettysburg at about 3 p.m. Hay's Brigade of Early's Confederate Division came on to the field and was unopposed. Early

gave him the order to keep advancing and not to stop until he hit the Federals. Hay's Brigade did just that; they rushed forward in extended order and about an hour and 4,000 yards later his somewhat winded but exhilarated brigade, along with Avery's Brigade, slammed into Coster's Union Brigade and routed it just outside of Gettysburg at the brickyard. If continuous movement is allowed, adopt the following rules.

Only Veteran or Elite active units, or Veteran or Elite unit groups in good order, may use continuous movements. At the start of its active turn, if a unit or unit group declares that for the its next two actions, it is doing nothing else – no firing, no formation change, no charge and is not forced to make a morale check of any kind – it gets an extra action of movement. However, it ends its turn in disorder and must roll a 1D6 for "stragglers." If the unit is forced to take any morale check while doing this, it does not get the extra movement, but still ends its turn in disorder and must still roll a 1D6 for "stragglers." Units in disorder or worse cannot use continuous movement.

STRAGGLERS

If called for by the scenario or if any unit uses continuous movement, that unit must roll a 1D6 at the end of its final movement for stragglers, in addition to now being in disorder. The number rolled with a 1D6 is the number of stragglers it has, and the rolled 1D6 die is placed by the unit to indicate how many stragglers there now are. This is a temporary reduction in the unit's figure count, but until the stragglers are recovered those figure losses are treated as "real," and negatively affect both a unit's Firepower Points (FPs) and its Basic Modified Morale Point (BMP) if the number of stragglers has caused the unit to lose a stand and reduced it to a depleted status.

STRAGGLING PENALTIES

If a unit with stragglers chooses to fire, its FPs are reduced by the number of stragglers it currently has. If a straggled unit is forced to take a morale check and the number of its stragglers has temporarily reduced it to less than one stand's worth of figures, the unit takes that specific morale check as a depleted unit. If a unit suffers casualties while it still has stragglers and if the combined straggler loss, previous losses and current fire loss is equal to or more than the figures the unit originally had, that unit is assumed to have disintegrated and is removed from the game. If a unit routs while still having stragglers, the temporary straggler figure loss is converted to a permanent figure loss.

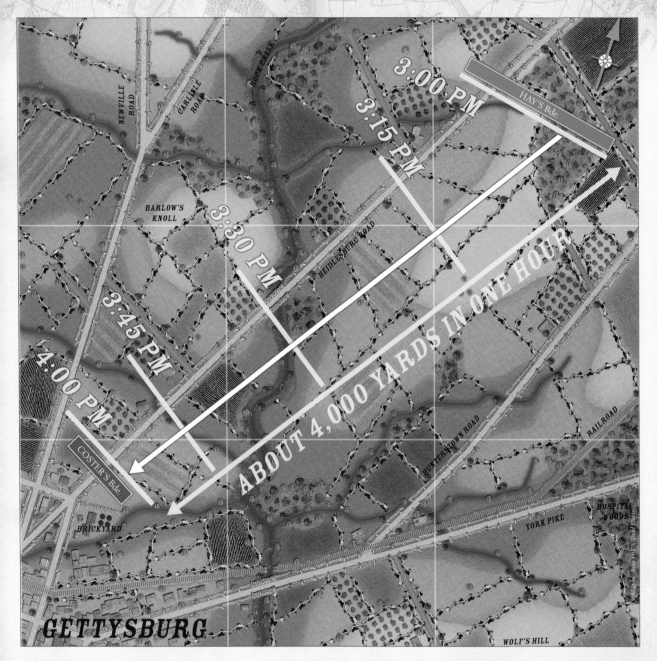

NEWVILLE ROAD

CARLISLE ROAD

ROCK CREEK

3:00 PM

HAY'S Bde.

3:15 PM

BARLOW'S KNOLL

HEIDLESBURG ROAD

3:30 PM

3:45 PM

ABOUT 4,000 YARDS IN ONE HOUR

4:00 PM

COSTER'S Bde.

HUNTERSTOWN ROAD

RAILROAD

BRICKYARD

YORK PIKE

HOSPITAL WOODS

GETTYSBURG

WOLF'S HILL

At the end of an hour, Hay's Brigade covered about 4,000 yards and would be part of a joint attack that would drive Coster's Brigade out of the "brickyard."

RECOVERING STRAGGLERS

To recover its stragglers, a disordered unit reforms back to good order by spending a reaction or action to reform, and rolls a 1D6 once to provide the number of stragglers it recovers (although never more than it lost). If the roll was less than the number that was lost, then the difference becomes a permanent loss. If a shaken unit has stragglers, it must first rally to good order before it can roll for straggler recovery. Routed units cannot roll for straggler recovery.

ARTILLERY BATTERY WITHDRAWAL

Experienced artillery crews learned that a risky but often effective way of pulling out of a difficult situation was to fire a full battery salvo and then, while its position was temporally covered with its own smoke, quickly limber and rapidly pull out. As with many such clever tactical expedients, sometimes it worked and sometimes it didn't. To offer artillery batteries this option, use the following optional rule.

Only Veteran and Elite batteries – not Green or Trained – may fire and then spend half a movement to limber and take a half limbered move away from the enemy, while covered by their own smoke. Such a move must be declared prior to doing it and can only be done as a combined two-action – fire & limber/move – turn. If so declared, any fire directed against the battery as it limbers and withdraws gets neither the -3 DRM benefit for being unlimbered nor the DRM penalties for being limbered. Any fire directed against the battery while this is being done is a dead even shot, with no DRM benefits or penalties. If one hit is scored against the retiring battery, the first hit is considered to be a horse hit. If two hits are scored against the retiring battery, then it is resolved as one horse hit and one section destroyed.

ARTILLERY FIRE OVER INFANTRY

Once the lines were established and if the terrain permitted it, the preferred Union defense was to move infantry up front along with a battery in direct support – usually Napoleons – to deliver point-blank canister fire into any attacking infantry. This would be supplemented with other artillery batteries – usually rifles – firing over the heads of the infantry with solid shot, shell or case shot so as to break up the attacking formations before they reached musket range. The Union batteries, having more reliable ammunition then their opponents, were consistently more comfortable firing over the heads of their own troops than were their Confederate counterparts. The rules for this are as follows:

Union artillery can do non-canister fire over the heads of friendly units if the battery or the targeted unit is at least one elevation higher than the intervening friendly unit, provided that both the firing battery and the targeted unit are at least two inches from the intervening friendly unit. Confederate batteries can also fire over friendly units in the same manner, but either the battery or the target must be at least two elevations higher than the intervening friendly unit and both the firing battery and the targeted unit have to be at least three inches from the intervening friendly unit.

Jones' artillery battalion deploys to support Jubal Early's division. (Patrick LeBeau & Chris Ward)

Union artillery at the battle of Malvern Hill, July 1, 1862, by Stephen Walsh © Osprey Publishing Ltd. Taken from Campaign 133: Seven Days Battles 1862.

OPTIONAL CANISTER EXCEPTION

While canister was very seldom fired over the heads of friendly infantry, it was occasionally done when in desperate situations. In the final defense of Seminary Ridge, Stevens' battery of six Napoleons would fire 57 rounds of canister directly over the heads of the 2nd and 7th Wisconsin regiments less than 80 yards away on the down slope. While the effect was staggering against the attacking Confederates, it also had an unsettling effect on the Union infantry underneath this canister storm. Lieutenant Colonel John Callis of the 7th Wisconsin claimed that he tried unsuccessfully to get the battery to stop, as it was killing some of his own men.

Long-range canister – but not point-blank canister – may be fired over the heads of friendly infantry as per all the regular rules for firing over friendly infantry. However, every time this is done the intervening friendly infantry must take a fired-on-rear by artillery (+4 to MMP) morale check. In any case, Union artillery can only do this if it has one elevation advantage, and Confederate artillery must continue to have a two-elevation advantage.

SHAKEN UNIT FORWARD MOVEMENT

Normally shaken units cannot move towards the enemy. However, it would be allowed if they had a leader attached and provided that the forward movement was all done behind non-skirmishing friendly units.

AREA FIRE

Any time there is a legitimate disagreement as to whether a unit can see a specific enemy unit or whether the visibility could be defined as obscured, then firing can still be allowed as area fire, which is done like any other fire but with one less die.

LEADER BENEFIT DIFFERENTIATION

Usually, if a leader is adjacent to a unit, his ability to improve movement and morale depends solely on his Leader Benefit (LB), which can be converted to extra inches of movement or a beneficial Modified Morale Point (MMP). If, and only if, a leader is actually attached to a unit, will that unit get a beneficial firing Die Roll Modifier (DRM). However, a case can be made that the ability of a leader to offer these benefits may actually depend on how involved he was with his brigade and/or one particular regiment. For example, just being seen nearby would probably be enough to bolster a unit's sagging morale, but to actually improve a regiment's firing might require his personal direction. To reflect these nuances more precisely, use the following rules:

EXTRA MOVEMENT

If a leader is attached to any one regiment and if all the regiments of that brigade are contiguously adjacent to the unit with the attached leader, when they move as a unit group, they would all get extra inches of movement equal to the leader's LB, provided the regiments remain adjacent to the leader or contiguously adjacent to a unit that is adjacent to him.

MORALE BENEFIT

If a leader is physically adjacent to a regiment, that regiment receives an MMP modifier equal to his leadership bonus. Depending on the actual unit configurations, it is possible that up to four adjacent regiments could receive this morale benefit.

FIRING BENEFIT

If, and only if, a leader is attached to a particular regiment can his LB be used to improve that one specific unit's firing as a beneficial DRM equal to the leader's LB. A leader can only benefit the firing of one unit or a single combined firing of adjacent units. However, the total combined FPs are still limited to 18 FPs for artillery, 16 FPs for infantry, and 14 FPs for cavalry.

ARTILLERY FIRING BENEFIT

All artillery leaders have an LB, which can help morale and extra limbered movement – not unlimbered movement – but only if an artillery leader has a specific (1 Artillery LB) can he help the artillery firing of a battery or battery group.

Howard attempts to rally XI Corps, by Adam Hook © Osprey Publishing Ltd. Taken from Campaign 55: Chancellorsville 1863.

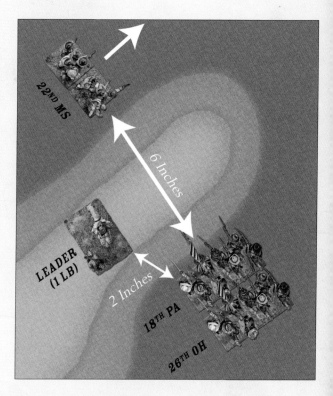

Any (1 LB) or better leader has a reaction radius equal to twice his LB rating in inches. So a (1 LB) leader would have a reaction radius of two inches. Then if that leader can see an enemy action he can order any one friendly unit or one unit group that is within his reaction radius to make a normal move or make a disordered charge. The leader would have to accompany the unit making the move or the disordered charge, and would have to roll for leader casualty.

Example: Normally, the 18th Philadelphia and 26th Ohio regiments could not react to the 22nd Mississippi Regiment moving across their front since the hill blocks their visibility and they cannot react to what they cannot see. However, since the leader can see the moving 22nd Mississippi, and the unit group of the 18th Philadelphia and 26th Ohio are within his reaction radius, he can order them to follow him and make a disordered charge over the hill and into the flank of the moving 22nd Mississippi. Even though the 26th Ohio is more than two inches away, it could join the charge since it is adjacent to and in the same formation as the 18th Philadelphia, and therefore is part of a legal unit group.

LEADER TRIGGERED REACTION

In most cases, a unit's legal reactions are limited to firing, re-forming, rallying, and with some restrictions, a counter-charge. For a unit to react to an enemy, that unit has to be able to see an enemy unit doing something, or if that unit can't see the enemy unit due to visibility restrictions, the reacting unit would have to be within two inches of it to react to it.

Normally, moving or charging is not a legal reaction. However, if a unit has a leader attached and either the unit or leader can see the "triggering" unit, or is within two inches of it, then that one unit may make a move or a charge as a legal reaction.

PLAYING ADF WITH 15MM *JOHNNY REB III* UNITS

Many gamers have their 15mm regiments mounted for *Johnny Reb III (JR III)*, and while they prefer the look of *JR III*'s larger 4-stand regiments, would like to use the *ADF* game mechanics, as *ADF* does away with the necessity of marking what each unit is going to do each and every turn. First, the 4-stand BMP morale chart will work nicely for the 4-stand regiments of *JR III*. The ground scale and turn time scales are close enough that it works for gaming purposes.

Since we would be using the *JR III* 4-stand units with one figure equaling 30 men, we will maintain the *JR III* 15mm ground scale of one inch equaling 50 yards, so that our scale regimental frontages stay the same. In *JR III* a battle line can move 6 inches (300 yards) in 20 minutes and can do a moving fire with one less die, while in *ADF* a 15mm battle line can also move 6 inches (300 yards in the JR III 15mm ground scale) in 30 minutes and then do only one fire action. In both game systems, moving fire is not as effective as a unit that is not moving and doing only firing. Of course, in *ADF* the regiment could choose not to fire and use both actions as movement actions, which would mean it has moved 600 yards in 30 minutes, but then it would have no active fire. The weapon ranges will be slightly different. At 50 yards per inch, in *JR III* the normal rifle-musket ranges is four inches or 200 yards, while in 15mm *ADF* (with the *JR III* 15mm scale) it is three inches or 150 yards. For firing, since you are "shooting" with twice as many figures, each shot will kill more figures, but since the target regiment also has more figures, the percentage of loss will be about the same per shot. There will be some anomalies, but no more than in any other wargame or in real battle itself.

SEQUENTIAL DISMOUNTED CAVALRY FIRE

When dismounted cavalry performs a point blank fire, it still gets to fire both its long weapon and its pistols, but not as one combined factor fire. Instead, they would fire their long weapons at short range, take a fear-of-charge morale check, and then fire their pistols at point blank range.

ALTERNATE 1:60 CAVALRY REPRESENTATION

When cavalry is deployed in less than a full regiment or brigade, the basic 1:30 figure ratio usually works best to portray those detached battalions. However, when entire cavalry regiments or brigades are deployed as entire units or when cavalry makes up the bulk of the battle force (such as at Brandy Station) or when they have been permanently dismounted, then a 1:60 ratio may work better. In that case, while they still might use cavalry weapons the troopers would then fire on the 1:60 infantry fire line.

EASTERN TERRAIN

THE ILLUSION OF SCALE

For all the scenarios in this book, the size of the grid squares on the scenario maps are defined by the figure scale that is being used as follows:

- For 6mm or 10mm figures, each map square is 12 inches across and each game board inch is about 100 to 120 yards.
- For 15mm or 20mm figures, each map square is 18 inches across and each game board inch is about 80 to 100 yards.
- For 25mm or 28mm figures, each map square is 24 inches across and each game board inch is about 60 to 80 yards.

All miniature wargames are an abstraction to some degree and many things are out-of-scale. There is a constant debate about how close to the ground scale the vertical scale should be and whether the buildings should be in scale with the ground scale or in scale with the figures. No matter how rigorous is the terrain replication, the game board will inevitably be a compromise, but it should be a compromise that creates the illusion that all elements are in scale with each other, even if they are not. Our miniature wargame tables are, at best, an impression of a historical battle, and the overall effect will not suffer provided the level of abstraction is consistent within each specific scenario or battle.

MODELING THE TERRAIN

SCALE AND ELEVATION

Most of the game boards for the Eastern Theater battles have from one to five relative elevations, with each elevation change representing approximately 20 to 30 feet of elevation difference. For example, the First Day of Gettysburg scenario boards have five elevation "levels," starting with Level 1 and going up to a Level 5, as indicated below. On that specific board, the top of Barlow's Knoll (Level 3) is roughly two elevation levels lower than where the Mummasburg Road crosses Oak Hill (level 5), and historically there was about a 50 to 60 foot elevation difference between the two points. Some individual aspects of a battlefield's terrain will often be unique and will require special rules. That, however, should not be considered a problem as "quirky terrain," such as the "Devil's Den" at Gettysburg, often conveys a unique tactical aspect when recreating a specific battle space.

When modeling the terrain, it is not necessary to portray each indicated level on the gaming board exactly as it is presented on the scenario map. Consider the scenario maps as guidelines that show which slopes were somewhat steeper than others and which hills were generally higher than others. Depending on the degree of replication or abstraction that is desired, just about any terrain modeling technique will work as long as the overall impression of the battlefield is presented in a generally consistent manner.

ELEVATION AND GOING UP SLOPE

With the exception of some steep river banks or abrupt slopes, most of the hills in these eastern scenarios were gentle rolling slopes that troops could easily go up or down without too much extra effort. However, there were always some significant exceptions. For instance, northwest of Gettysburg the east slope of Oak Hill was

LEVEL 5 (Oak Hill)
LEVEL 4 (Herr Ridge)
LEVEL 3 (Seminary Ridge)
LEVEL 2
LEVEL 1
LEVEL 0

Heavy Woods
Light Woods
Farms & Orchards
Rock Creek

much steeper than the west slope. Consequently, there is no extra movement penalty for troops going up or down a slope unless the unit is moving up a steep slope, which is defined as going up two elevation differences in any one movement action, as follows:

If a unit is moving up two different elevation levels or their equivalent during any one movement action, then the movement rate is done at one terrain type worse than it normally would be. For example, should a unit be moving through light woods and going up a slope of two

elevation differences, that movement would be done at the heavy woods movement rate.

ELEVATION AND LINE OF SIGHT

There are two major scenery modeling techniques that wargamers use when portraying elevation differences and for determining the impact of intervening hills, knolls, or other sight-blocking objects, such as farms or woods. One is the contoured terrain method, where each of the major game elevation contours is portrayed as a distinct level so

The contour terrain method makes it very easy to determine which units are on a slope and which are not. Depending on the scenario, the sloping hill that the two Confederate brigades are attacking could be plausibly defined as either a Level Two or Level Three Hill. (Malcolm Johnston)

that there is no debate as to which elevation a unit is on, and who might be able to fire over whom. The other approach, known as flex terrain, is where the gaming surface is portrayed with a thin flexible rug or the equivalent so as to create model terrain with gently rolling hills and valleys that seamlessly blend together. Nevertheless, given the fact that even the smaller 6mm or 10mm figures are greatly out of scale with most wargame ground scales, significant abstraction is usually necessary in simulating the Line-of-Sight (LOS) impact of the miniature terrain, no matter which modeling method is used.

Contoured terrain can either be made with layers of Styrofoam cut roughly to the shape of the actual terrain contours so as to make a permanent miniature board of the historical terrain, or it can take the shape of removable individual hills that approximate the shape of the desired hills, which then can also be used for other scenarios. If contoured terrain is used, then the First Day of Gettysburg terrain map with its five

indicated levels can serve as a general guide for the respective heights and slopes of the different levels. With that in mind, the diagram and table below should be taken as a relative guide to the terrain and how elevation differences impact a unit's LOS rather than as a strict elevation definition of each level being so many feet high. In scaling these levels to the wargame table, assume that one level of terrain corresponds to roughly the height of most farm buildings and orchards, while light woods are twice that and heavy woods are triple that. This will look even better if the buildings used are one scale less than the figures, so if you play with 25mm or 28mm figures, consider using 15mm or even 10mm buildings, as they will look just as good and their footprint will be closer in scale to the ground scale. Since the vertical scale is almost always exaggerated on a typical wargame table, a case can be made for using the lower ½ inch per each level, even for the larger 15mm-sized figures – it all depends on personal preference and the terrain effect you are trying to capture.

Hill Height above Level 1				
Figure Size	Level 2	Level 3	Level 4	Level 5
6mm/10mm	½ inch	¾ inch	1 inch	2 inches
15mm/20mm	¾ inch	1½ inches	2 inches	3 inches
25mm/28mm	1 inch	2 inches	3 inches	4 inches

The above hill guidelines assume that each 6mm/10mm level is approximately ½ inch, each 15mm/20mm level is about ¾ inch and each 25mm/28mm level is about 1 inch. However, given the wide variety in the height of even standardized figure heights, it is quite possible that for any given wargame table a different elevation value per level might look better. For example, for 15mm figures use either ½ inch per level or ¾ inch per level, whichever looks better to you.

So, a unit on the top of Herr Ridge (Level 4) could see, to some degree, over farms, orchards and light

woods, but heavy woods would hide anything behind them. However, even if a unit is higher than a potential blocking object and could technically see over it, the area directly behind such an object would still have a shadow area or dead ground that would not be visible. Even a small stretch of dead ground can have a significant tactical effect, as in the Battle of Piedmont scenario. As might be expected, taller objects would have a larger shadow than shorter objects, and a high hill has a longer shadow than a low hill. A rough guide to this shadow effect for contoured terrain is suggested in the table below.

Line-of-Sight Shadow Effect				
Figure Size	Farms & Orchards	Light Woods	Heavy Woods	Hill Height*
6mm/10mm	1 inch	2 inches	3 inches	¾ inch per level
15mm/20mm	2 inches	3 inches	4 inches	1 inch per level
25mm/28mm	3 inches	4 inches	5 inches	1½ inches per level
* Hill Height is defined as the number of levels above Level 1: so a Level 3 hill is two levels high.				

Flex terrain mimics the subtle slopes of many a civil war battlefield. (Dean West)

For example, in the previous diagram should a 15mm battery on Seminary Ridge (Level 3) want to fire at a target just beyond the orchard, it could only do so if the target was more than two inches beyond the edge of the orchard, because if it was closer than two inches from the orchard's edge, the LOS shadow of the orchard would prevent the battery from seeing it.

If flex terrain is used, a pliable gaming surface such as a thin rug with all the major terrain areas painted or flocked onto it can be draped over various shapes of approximately the correct heights to create the impression of gentle rolling hills that seamlessly flow into each other. Flex terrain has the visual advantage that the resulting terrain has more natural undulations, which are typical of the Virginia, Pennsylvania and Maryland countryside that saw the vast majority of the eastern fighting.

Flex terrain can have the disadvantage that it can be more difficult to determine which relative level a unit might be on, or to easily discern if a certain battery can fire over a specific battle line. However, as illustrated below, a same-sized dice or standardized block – perhaps equal to the equivalent of one level – can be used to indicate a standard target height or object height. Then a long ruler or straight edge is laid from the top of the shooter's block across the intervening object or hill and to the intended target block to determine the shadow area. If the ruler or straight edge can touch the top of the shooter's block and the target's block, then the shooter has a legal LOS. In the example below, the small knoll blocks visibility to target A, but not to target B, so a hilltop battery could see and fire on target B. To determine LOS over other blocking terrain such as a farm complex or light woods, small standardized blocks could be fashioned to indicate the relative true game height of each of these objects, and used in the same manner to determine which blocking terrain can be seen over and which cannot.

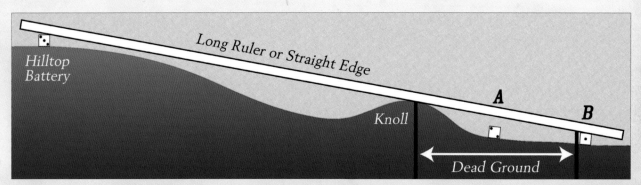

Height of Standardized Blocks for Visibility Determination				
Figure Size	Target Units	Farms & Orchards	Light Woods	Heavy Woods
6mm/10mm	½ inch	¾ inch	1 inch	1½ inches
15mm/20mm	¾ inch	1 inch	1½ inches	2 inches
25mm/28mm	1 inch	1½ inches	2 inches	2½ inches

ELEVATION AND VISIBILITY DISTANCE

On a 19th-century battlefield obscured with the dust of thousands of men, animals and dense layers of black powder smoke, holding the high ground could give units a distinct visibility advantage. Technological advances in the effective range of rifled artillery could be largely negated if targets could not be seen and identified. However, even a modest height advantage could enable experienced commanders and gunners to see over the smoky chaos and engage targets at much longer ranges than was practical in earlier wars. The visibility advantage of Cemetery Hill was probably one of the main reasons the Union would eventually put 12 batteries almost hub-to-hub along its crest, and while Big Round Top was certainly the highest point on the battlefield, it had questionable military value since it was covered with heavy woods that tended to nullify much of its potential visibility advantage. The following table shows the visibility advantage of the high ground and how far a unit can see from each of the different elevation levels.

Maximum Visibility in inches (10mm / 15mm / 25mm)			
Unit Sighting	Morning	Afternoon	Night
From Level 1 or 2	20 / 24 / 28	16 / 20 / 24	12 / 16 / 20
From Level 3 or 4	24 / 28 / 32	20 / 24 / 28	16 / 20 / 24
From Level 5 or 6	28 / 32 / 36	24 / 28 / 32	20 / 24 / 28

For all the scenarios in this book unless specified otherwise, morning is up to and including the 12 noon turn and afternoon is from 12.30 p.m. up to and including the 7 p.m. turn. All turns from the 7.30 p.m. turn on are considered as night turns.

If a unit wishes to fire at an enemy unit that is beyond visibility, it can still do so, but it would be considered to be "area fire" and would cost the shooter one less die. It is certainly possible that an artillery battery on higher ground (level 3, 4 or 5) than an opposing artillery battery on lower ground (level 1 or 2) would have full visibility, while the battery on the lower elevation would be forced to fire back with area fire and consequently would be rolling one fewer die than its opposing battery on the higher ground. In such a case, the guns on the high ground would definitely have an advantage. The height or visibility advantage would certainly have been one possible factor on the afternoon of July 2 at Gettysburg, when combined Confederate gun battalions on Benner's Hill attempted to engage the Union batteries on Cemetery Hill, a somewhat higher position. After about two hours, it became clear that the Federal gunners were winning and the Confederates began to withdraw their guns from Benner's Hill.

TERRAIN DETAILS

Given the large ground scale of *Across a Deadly Field*, a better battlefield impression is usually created if the buildings are at least one size smaller than the figure size. If using 15mm figures where one inch is about 80 to 100 yards, 10mm or even 6mm buildings often have a footprint that is closer to consistency with the game's ground scale than would most 15mm buildings. Also, *Across a Deadly Field* does not recommend trying to model every building in a farm complex, but rather suggests that the farm area be defined by a fenced-in area with a single farm-like building. This will define where a farm area is and where it is not, while still leaving plenty of room for the figures. Our miniature wargame tables are, at best, an illusion of a historical battle and that illusion will not suffer from greater or fewer abstractions provided the level of abstraction is consistent within each specific scenario or battle.

If a unit is in a built-up farm area – an enclosed fenced area with a building in it – the target unit gets a -1 DRM from artillery fire and a -3 DRM from infantry fire, but no additional benefit from the surrounding fences. Units in a farm area receive the -1 MMP cover morale benefit for being in cover against all fires. LOS extends into a farm or orchard area, but not through it.

When firing from within a farm or town area, a unit's FPs are halved – unless it is exactly on the edge – against a unit outside the farm area.

LIGHT AND HEAVY WOODS

Eastern woods could either be light woods or heavy woods, with the difference usually being determined by the proximity of the woods to active farm areas. When the wooded areas were adjacent or near the farms, the domestic animals were often left to wander through them to seek shade from the summer sun and to graze on the

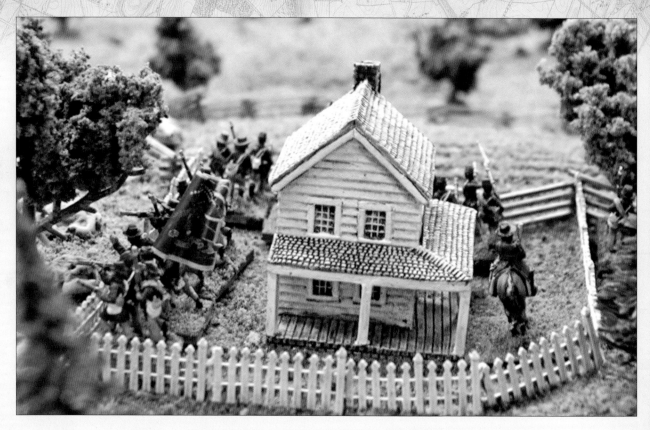

A 15mm Union brigade of four regiments defends a 10mm fenced farm area. (Doug Kline)

grasses and brush under the trees. The net result was that over a few seasons, the undergrowth of the forest would be cleaned out while the farmers themselves would chop down the smaller trees for fence rails and firewood. With the undergrowth thinned or cleared out, movement was easier and visibility was better. The heavier woods were usually in areas that were too wild, rugged or steep for the animals to graze and consequently the undergrowth often became a tangle of small trees and tough vines.

Visibility determination is different for heavy and light woods. Units outside heavy woods can only see a target if it is on the edge of the heavy woods. However, units outside light woods can see into one inch of light woods. If two opposing units are in heavy woods they can only see up to one inch through the woods. However, they could still do area fire in heavy woods out to a maximum distance of two inches. If two opposing units are in light woods, roll a 1D6 for visibility before each fire; this will give the visibility in inches, up to a maximum of three inches, or up to a maximum of four inches for area fire in

light woods. If two opposing units are in heavy woods, the procedure is the same except that the all distances are defined as half inches, with a maximum visibility for heavy woods being one inch or two inches for area fire. For both heavy and light woods of any size, there is no visibility completely through the woods to an opposing unit on the opposite side of the woods.

THE EASTERN ROADS

In rural Virginia, Maryland and Pennsylvania, there were two road types, the main macadam or gravel roads and the many smaller farm roads that were usually dirt. The more rural the area, the more the dirt roads were the norm. The main roads were usually bordered by heavy rail and post fences and were named, though the names

The battle of the Wilderness, by Gerry Embleton © Osprey Publishing Ltd. Taken from Warrior 6: Confederate Infantryman 1861–65.

could vary depending on location. For game purposes the main or named roads should be treated as roads for movement, and the farm roads should use the trail movement category.

A MULTITUDE OF FENCES

Many of the eastern agricultural areas had wooden fences of every possible type, and based on the best historical estimates the scenario maps indicate their most likely locations. Some agricultural areas such as those in Pennsylvania seemed to have fences everywhere; other areas, such as parts of more rural Virginia, had much less. In any case, it is not necessary to model each and every fence. As noted, the heavier wood fences were usually found along the named roads and pikes, such as the Chambersburg Pike. Should you have a limited model fence inventory, those should be simulated first. The lighter split-rail fences were commonly used around the individual fields and farms, and an acceptable representation of the fenced fields of Gettysburg could be accomplished by simply modeling every other fence. In any case, the fence rules are as follows:

Any movement across one or more fences or stone walls is done at the broken terrain movement rate. If limbered artillery or an infantry column crosses any fence or stone wall, a gap in the fence is immediately created at that point. If a unit in line or extended line – not skirmishers – crosses a light wooden fence, it is assumed they have knocked it down as they crossed. A heavy wood fence or a stone wall, however, has to be climbed over at the broken terrain rate and it is assumed to remain, unless a gap was created by a column of infantry, cavalry or limbered artillery as noted above.

ORCHARDS

The Maryland, Virginia and Pennsylvania farmers loved their orchards, and while some were bigger than others it was a rare farm that did not have even a small one. Indeed, many orchards would become famous as the focal point of a particular struggle, such as the peach orchards at Shiloh or the second day of Gettysburg.

Orchards are treated as broken terrain for movement and block LOS if a unit is trying to see completely through them. Orchards, however, have no LOS impediment to seeing into them. Orchards provide a -1 DRM target benefit from infantry fire, but no benefit from artillery fire. Any unit in an orchard is entitled to the -1 MMP cover morale benefit against infantry fire, but not from artillery fire.

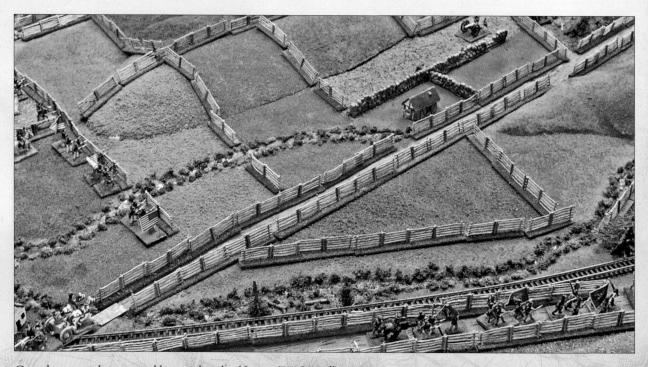

Gettysburg was characterized by a multitude of fences. (P.J. O'Neill)

THE FIRST DAY OF GETTYSBURG SCENARIO SET

JULY 1, 1863

The first day of the Battle of Gettysburg has been the subject of countless books and studies because it might have been the best chance Robert E. Lee had to win the war in an afternoon. If a Union defeat had been serious enough to force the Army of the Potomac to retreat to an already identified defensive position along Pipe Creek, the political repercussions of such an event might have been sufficient to force President Lincoln to accept a negotiated peace with the Confederacy. The first day of battle offered the Confederate Army of Northern Virginia its best chance of accomplishing that, as the Union forces arrived piecemeal. Furthermore, the first day would be the only day that the Confederates would have a significant artillery superiority. By the afternoon of July 2, the second day of the battle, the arrival of the Army of the Potomac's reserve artillery – 114 guns in five brigades – and the later advent of the powerful VI Corps made a decisive Confederate victory problematic at best. On the third day, the grand charge – known forever as Pickett's Charge – would prove to be as hopeless as it was gallant as it advanced into the converging fire of about a hundred guns.

A MUDDLED CONCENTRATION

In the late afternoon of June 28, Lieutenant General James Longstreet brought his trusted spy Harrison to General Robert E. Lee's headquarters to brief Lee on the latest locations of the seven corps of the Army of the Potomac. The news that the Federal Army was relatively close and concentrated around Frederick, Maryland was unexpected, as Lee had assumed that they were still across the Potomac in Virginia. In response, Lee immediately started issuing orders for his army to concentrate. It was not a problem for his I and III Corps, as they were both gathered in the Chambersburg area.

Pickett's Charge, by Adam Hook © Osprey Publishing Ltd. Taken from Campaign 52: Gettysburg 1863.

However, Lee's II Corps under Lieutenant General Richard Ewell was much further advanced, with Rodes' and Johnson's divisions preparing to move against Harrisburg, while Early's division was further east at York. Since the bulk of the army was already at Chambersburg, Lee's initial June 28 order was to have Ewell's II Corps fall back and join the rest of the army at Chambersburg. With considerable complaining, Ewell started to comply and immediately sent Johnson's division, II Corps' reserve artillery and much of the II Corps' train southwest on the road to Chambersburg.

By the morning of June 29, however, Lee had reconsidered and sent Ewell a new order directing him to concentrate the II Corps at Cashtown or Gettysburg, as "circumstances might dictate." This further upset General Ewell, who sputtered that Lee needed someone on his staff who could write an intelligible order. In a huff, Ewell ordered Early's division to move west from York and Rodes' division to move south from Carlisle so as to

converge near Gettysburg. However, no new orders were sent to General Johnson, who continued with his original order to move towards Chambersburg. Eventually, Johnson and the II Corps reserve artillery would turn east at Scotland and then would interpose themselves into the already congested III Corps line of march, creating a monumental traffic jam at Greenwood, just west of the narrow Cashtown Gap. This may have been the critical Confederate administrative mistake of the Gettysburg campaign, since it would not only delay Johnson's division in re-joining II Corps, but would also delay Anderson's, Hood's and McLaw's divisions by up to five hours in reaching the battlefield. Had this not occurred and had Johnson's division been ordered to counter-march and simply follow Rodes south to Gettysburg, then both Anderson's and Johnson's division could almost certainly have been available for the later stages of the July 1 battle at Gettysburg. If generals Lee, Ewell or their staffs had paid more attention to traffic control, road capacities and

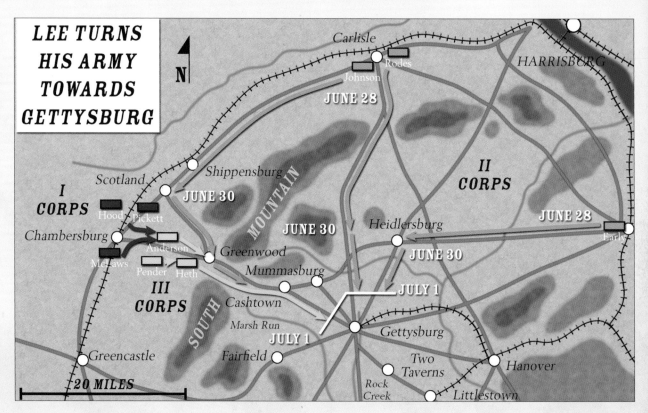

Late on June 28 Lee ordered his army to concentrate at Chambersburg, but by the morning of June 29, he instructed Ewell's II Corps to concentrate instead either at Cashtown or Gettysburg. However, no new orders were sent to Johnson's division, which continued to march westward and eventually created a monumental traffic jam outside Cashtown Gap, delaying Anderson's division along with Hood's and McLaw's divisions of Longstreet's Corps for about five hours.

Jubal Early faces off against the just-arrived 1st Division of the Union XII Corps. (Patrick LeBeau & Chris Ward)

lines of march, both Anderson's division of A. P. Hill's III Corps and Johnson's division of II Corps could have joined the first day's fight. For this reason they are included in the Confederate Orders of Battle for July 1 and in some of the scenarios should the gamer wish to explore that "what if" option.

HISTORICAL RESTRAINTS AND THE FOG OF WAR

In any historical battle situation there were inevitable restraints that contributed to the opposing commander's decisions. When the military historian reviews these battles, he has almost perfect intelligence as to the forces each side had, and when and where those forces would be arriving. We look down on our miniature battlefields, and even if the players are using hidden movement we can almost instantly appreciate where the natural lines of defense and offensive avenues of approach are likely to be. There is no major unknown factor or one nagging intelligence report that may or may not be accurate but, if ignored, could be

critical to winning or losing the battle. On the smoke-filled civil war battlefield, commanders from regimental to senior army level were constantly making decisions based on fragmentary or even wrong information. The "fog of war" creates hesitancy and caution, so it is very understandable that these leaders would hold substantial units back as a reserve in case the decision that they just made or are about to make would absolutely be the wrong thing to do. These uncertainties were very real for the two opposing commanders as their armies marched towards Gettysburg. For Robert E. Lee, a decisive defeat deep in northern soil could result in his entire army being destroyed, along with any hope of southern independence. For George Meade, who had only been in command of the Army of the Potomac for five days, the political repercussions of a decisive defeat of the Union's premier fighting force on its home soil could have been the psychological blow that might have forced President Lincoln to accept an accommodation with the Confederacy.

ARMIES APPROACHING GETTYSBURG - A CLIMATE OF UNCERTAINTY

In each of the July 1 Gettysburg scenarios, the historical restraints – good, bad or indifferent – are pointed out and the gamers can decide to play with them or not, or even let a random roll of the die determine which units do or do not participate. For the Confederates, overshadowing almost of all of the divisional and corps commanders' decisions that first day was General Lee's desire, which he had made very clear, that he did not want to bring on a general engagement until his army was concentrated and he had definitive information as to the location of the Union Army. These factors almost certainly weighed on Lee's decision to keep much of the combat power of the Confederate III Corps then advancing down the Chambersburg Pike held back as a reserve against the unexpected. The III Corps units that were held back on the first day were R. H. Anderson's entire division (7,000 men, 17 guns), Thomas' Brigade of W. D. Pender's division (1,300 men), most of Garnett's artillery battalion (15 guns) and Pogue's artillery battalion (16 guns). In addition to holding these forces back, the Confederate attacks against the Union I Corps were hesitant. From 12 p.m. until a little after 2 p.m. there were no significant attacks against the Federals, only artillery exchanges. In addition, the bulk of Pegram's and McIntosh's excellent artillery battalions were not brought forward even after their primary target, the Federals on McPherson's Ridge, had been driven off. Hence the final Confederate assault against the battered but defiant Union I Corps holding tight on Seminary Ridge was done without artillery support. It is, however, unclear if that was by choice or simply an oversight.

The Army of the Potomac's new commander, Major General George Meade, had his own uncertainty issue that created some confusion among his corps commanders as to his intention. Meade's overall concept of operation for July 1 was sound enough. The I and XI Corps under General Reynolds would support Buford's cavalry at Gettysburg, with III Corps supporting Reynolds' left flank at Emmitsburg and XII Corps his right flank at Two Taverns. However, then Meade clouded the issue with his "Pipe Creek Circular," which was sent to all his corps commanders (although his most important commander, Major General John Reynolds, did not get it). This appeared to detail Meade's preferred battle plan: a defensive stand along Pipe Creek southeast of Gettysburg. It was a lengthy document detailing the routes of march and the final positions of each corps.

Since most of Meade's corps commanders now believed that this would eventually be where Meade wanted the battle to be fought, there was an understandable hesitancy to rush everything forward to Gettysburg, since they then would have to retrace their steps back to Pipe Creek. The Pipe Creek option certainly played a role in Major General Henry Slocum's decision not to move the XII Corps forward to Gettysburg, but to wait for developments for over three hours at Two Taverns, barely five miles from Gettysburg.

There were also conflicting orders. General Meade ordered the army's III Corps under Major General Daniel Sickles to halt and hold the corps in readiness at Emmitsburg – the western approach to the Pipe Creek position. However, Sickles' immediate superior General Reynolds, the left wing commander, had ordered Sickles to bring the entire III Corps immediately to Gettysburg just moments before Reynolds was shot dead. Sickles would eventually compromise and bring four of his six brigades to Gettysburg that evening, while leaving two behind at Emmitsburg. However, had Sickles immediately followed his gut instinct to march at that moment to the sound of the guns, his entire corps would have arrived by mid-afternoon to help hold back the Confederate onslaught. As was mentioned, these historical options and restraints are all reflected in these scenarios, but are duly noted so the gamer can explore some alternative and very interesting "what ifs."

THE FIRST DAY OF GETTYSBURG SCENARIO SET

The First Day of Gettysburg Scenario Set is composed of the "Along the Chambersburg Pike" series of three scenarios: "The Devil to Pay", "McPherson's Ridge," and "Seminary Ridge." These can be played as individual historical snapshot scenarios or one long continuous scenario, "Along the Chambersburg Pike". The First Day set also includes two other scenarios, "Barlow's Knoll" and "If Slocum Wasn't Slow," which use the middle and eastern boards respectively. Both of those can be played with either a 2 p.m. or 3 p.m. historical start time. Either version of these two scenarios can also be combined with the "McPherson's Ridge" scenario into one large scenario, "A Long Afternoon," which combines all three scenarios and covers the critical entire late afternoon fighting of the first day from about 2 p.m. to 6 p.m. to form one large grand convention-sized scenario.

THE FIRST DAY OF GETTYSBURG - SCENARIO SET

"A LONG AFTERNOON" - Combines "McPherson's Ridge", "Barlow's Knoll - 2 PM Start" and "Slocum Arrives - 2 PM Start" - from 2:00 PM to 6:00 PM.

"A VERY LONG DAY" - Is the entire first day with the same forces as above, but without some of the historical restraints - from 8:00 AM to 6:00 PM.

"A VERY TOUGH DAY" - Assumes that neither side repeats their initial historical mistakes and both bring in all the forces that could have been there on July 1, 1863. For the Confederates this includes Johnson's and Anderson's Divisions and for the Union it would include all of III Corps and all of XII Corps.

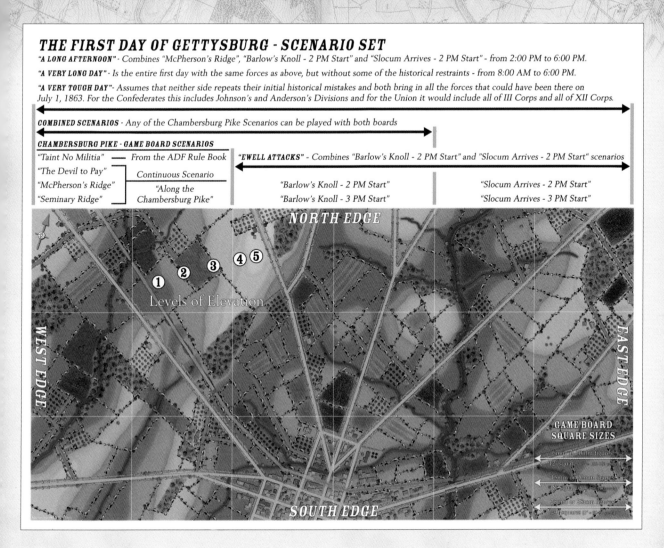

COMBINED SCENARIOS - Any of the Chambersburg Pike Scenarios can be played with both boards

CHAMBERSBURG PIKE - GAME BOARD SCENARIOS

"Taint No Militia"	── From the ADF Rule Book	**"EWELL ATTACKS"** - Combines "Barlow's Knoll - 2 PM Start" and "Slocum Arrives - 2 PM Start" scenarios
"The Devil to Pay"	Continuous Scenario	
"McPherson's Ridge"	"Along the	"Barlow's Knoll - 2 PM Start"	"Slocum Arrives - 2 PM Start"
"Seminary Ridge"	Chambersburg Pike"	"Barlow's Knoll - 3 PM Start"	"Slocum Arrives - 3 PM Start"

NORTH EDGE

WEST EDGE

EAST EDGE

Levels of Elevation

GAME BOARD SQUARE SIZES

SOUTH EDGE

The "A Very Long Day" scenario covers all the serious fighting of the first day from 8 a.m. to 6 p.m. and all the historically available units, but without some of the historical hesitations that hampered both sides. For the Confederates, this scenario removes the historical 12 noon to 2 p.m. lull in which there were no attacks, only artillery firing. For the Union, it has some of the III Corps units arriving sooner than they did, as General Reynolds had originally requested just before he was shot.

The "A Very Tough Day" scenario also covers all the serious fighting of the first day from 8 a.m. to 6 p.m. without the historical delay and the mid-day lull. In addition, it offers the wargamer the opportunity to explore the probable results of neither side making the administrative missteps that they historically did. For the Confederates, this means that Johnson's division follows Rodes' division into the battle and Lee releases Anderson's division rather than holding it back in reserve. For the Union, it would mean that all of Slocum's XII Corps and Sickle's III Corps immediately move to the sound of the guns rather than waiting for specific clarifying orders from General Meade.

Despite their large scope, "A Long Afternoon", "A Very Long Day" and "A Very Tough Day" scenarios do not require excessive table space. A 6mm or 10mm game will only require a 3-foot by 6-foot space, a 15mm game will fill a 5-foot by 9-foot table, and a 25mm or 28mm game will need a 6-foot by 12-foot table, all of which is very manageable in a club or convention environment. This combined scenario focuses on the entire late afternoon battle north of Gettysburg and can

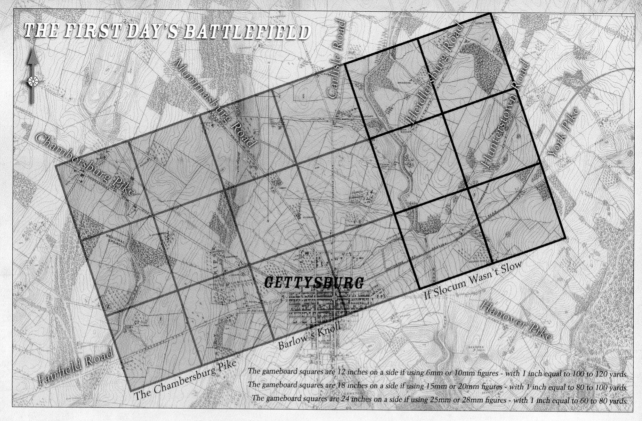

THE FIRST DAY'S BATTLEFIELD

GETTYSBURG

If Slocum Wasn't Slow

Barlow's Knoll

The Chambersburg Pike

Fairfield Road

The gameboard squares are 12 inches on a side if using 6mm or 10mm figures - with 1 inch equal to 100 to 120 yards.
The gameboard squares are 18 inches on a side if using 15mm or 20mm figures - with 1 inch equal to 80 to 100 yards.
The gameboard squares are 24 inches on a side if using 25mm or 28mm figures - with 1 inch equal to 60 to 80 yards.

The overlay indicates the area covered by the three wargame tables that are used for the individual first day of Gettysburg scenarios. When all three tables are put together, the combined first day of Gettysburg scenarios take a 5x9-foot table if using the 15mm figure ground scale of one inch equals approximately 80 to 100 yards. The original map was done by Brevet Major General G. K. Warren, Chief of Engineers of the Army of the Potomac in 1868. (US Library of Congress)

be played as a strictly historical recreation or can include all the units that could have been there had their respective commanders – including both Meade and Lee – not hesitated or better coordinated their army's approach to the battlefield. For the Confederates, that could have included Johnson's division of the II Corps and Anderson's division of the III Corps. For the Union, that would have included the two divisions of Slocum's XII Corps and almost all of Sickles' III Corps.

For the gamers that like to build specific game boards, all three of the historical scenarios of the "Along the Chambersburg Pike" series use the same board, with each battle providing an exciting two- or three-hour battle, or the situation can be played as one continuing scenario. Almost all of the fighting along the Chambersburg Pike was a fight between the Army of the Potomac's I Corps under Major General John Reynolds, who was trying to

hold off the Army of Northern Virginia's III Corps under Lieutenant General A. P. Hill. Other units from adjacent commands – such as Daniels' Brigade from Rodes' Division – would certainly play a role, but this was basically a stand-up fight between these two opposing infantry corps.

THE TERRAIN - NORTH OF GETTYSBURG
The terrain north of Gettysburg was defined by Oak Hill in the west and by Rock Creek in the east. From both east and west – up until Oak Hill – the terrain slopes gradually downward to Rock Creek with a few undulations, bumps and knolls along the way. Almost all of the wooded patches have been thinned by farmers and grazing animals, so except for a few very rugged areas directly adjacent to Rock Creek all the woods should be considered as light woods. In the west, the

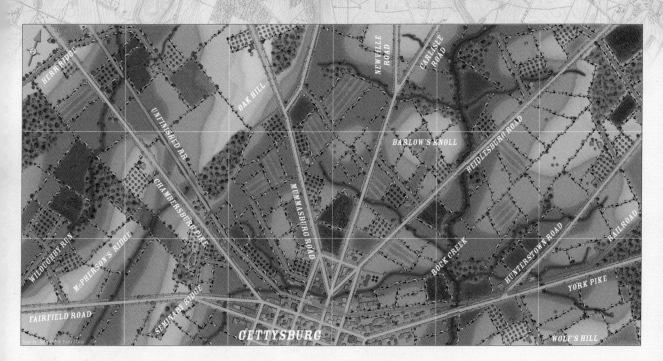

singular terrain feature is Oak Hill. It continues to rise north of the Mummasburg Road, eventually reaching an off-board wooded height of 520 feet. The two famous defensive ridges of Gettysburg – McPherson's Ridge and Seminary Ridge – are both gradually descending ridge-lines of Oak Hill.

CREEKS, STREAMS, RUNS AND WOODS

Rock Creek was probably the only watercourse in the Gettysburg area that was an impediment to orderly maneuver. Despite having been victorious with his attack, General Gordon later commented that "crossing the creek ... the banks were so abrupt as to prevent a passage except at certain points ... the enemy made a most obstinate resistance."

Rock Creek is treated as one inch of heavy woods for infantry or cavalry movement and one inch of rough terrain for artillery movement. Infantry in or crossing Rock Creek are in disorder. If an infantry or cavalry unit attempts to fire while in Rock Creek it suffers an extra -4 DRM firing detriment to all its fires. Artillery may not fire while in Rock Creek. If a unit is targeted while in Rock Creek, the firer gets an extra +4 DRM firing benefit. A unit in Rock Creek has its maximum visibility limited to two inches in all directions. However, the small streams and runs only cost one inch extra to cross, or nothing extra if the whole move is made as if in broken terrain. Any wooded area adjacent to Rock Creek

is defined as heavy woods within ½ inch of Rock Creek, but beyond ½ inch it is light woods. Any unit in either light or heavy woods is entitled to the -1 MMP cover morale benefit.

RAILROADS, GRADES AND RAILROAD CUTS

On the Gettysburg map is a finished railroad, an unfinished railroad grade and three railroad cuts across the ridges that radiate south from Oak Hill, just west of Gettysburg. The west cut across McPherson's Ridge was the deepest and the most famous, as that was where 225 Confederates of the 2nd and 42nd Mississippi regiments were trapped and forced to surrender by the 6th Wisconsin and the 95th New York regiments. The rules for the railroads and the railroad cuts are as follows:

The railroad, the unfinished railroad grade, and the railroad cuts are treated as open terrain for column or limbered movement along or through them. There is no extra movement or combat penalty for units moving across the railroad or the unfinished railroad grade. Moving across the railroad cuts, however, is treated as moving across one inch of rough terrain. Infantry units in a railroad cut are either in a column or disorder and artillery can only be limbered. If an infantry or cavalry unit attempts to fire while in a railroad cut, it suffers an extra -4 DRM firing detriment to all its fires. Artillery may only fire one section while in a railroad cut, and that fire is limited to along the railroad cut. If a unit is targeted

Pender's Division forms up for its attack against the Union I Corps. (Patrick LeBeau & Chris Ward)

while in Rock Creek, the firer gets an extra +4 DRM firing bonus for firing at a unit in the railroad cut.

SCENARIO SETUP

Most of the scenario maps show a designated brigade area where the regiments or battalions of that brigade may set up in within that area in either battle line or extended line, unless the map indicates that they enter in road column. If desired, each brigade of four or fewer regiments may have one regiment advanced two inches forward as skirmishers, and one regiment two inches back as a reserve. If a brigade has five or more regiments, it may advance up to two regiments two inches forward as skirmishers and one regiment two inches back as a reserve. If a regimental rather than a brigade position is indicated, that is where at least one stand of the regiment must be placed and the regiment can be placed in skirmish, extended line or battle line.

SCENARIO UNIT DESIGNATIONS

As an administrative practice, the Army of the Potomac and Army of Northern Virginia used slightly different official systems of brigade designation. The Union preferred to list their brigades with a numerical designation of brigade number, division number, and then corps number. In that system, Meredith's "Iron Brigade" would officially be referred to as the First Brigade, First Division, I Corps, or simply as the "1-1-1" brigade. Likewise, the Federals listed their batteries by their official unit declension, such as the 1st Rhode Island, Battery C. The Confederates tended to be more informal and simply referred to the divisions, brigades and batteries by the names of their commander. However, there were exceptions. Some Confederate brigades would often retain the name of an earlier charismatic commander even after he was gone. For instance, Brigadier General Robert Hoke's original North Carolina brigade was commanded by Colonel Isaac Avery throughout the Gettysburg campaign, but the brigade was still commonly referred to as Hoke's Brigade. In any case, for the sake of consistency of scenario description and ease of setup, the Confederate system will be used to identify brigades and batteries. Hence, on the scenario setup map, the XI Corps Brigade, "2-3-11," will simply be shown and identified as "Krzyzanowski's Brigade."

GENERALS LEE AND MEADE

In all the first day of Gettysburg scenarios there is no need to have a specific Lee or Meade figure, as their individual figures will play no role in the scenarios. Meade would not arrive until about just after midnight that evening, and though Lee would arrive on Herr Ridge by mid-afternoon, his tactical involvement in the first day's battle was minimal. Lee at that time was not at his best. He, as we now know, was still recovering from an earlier heart attack and continued to suffer from lingering dysentery. He was also faced with a situation he had not experienced before, an almost total lack of reliable intelligence on the location of his opponent, the Army of the Potomac. That issue, when coupled with his degraded health, resulted in Lee becoming hesitant to commit his forces to a battle before his army was united. In essence, he may have been little more than an interested observer as events unfolded on July 1. Nevertheless, the effect of Lee's presence on the field is reflected in specific scenario rules, such as to which side is defined as having the initiative or by giving the Confederates the advantage in tied initiative die roll.

THE OPPOSING FORCES

ARMY COMPARISON

The two armies that maneuvered to a collision at Gettysburg were either adjusting to major new command positions or substantial organizational changes. Major General George Meade had only been command of the Army of the Potomac for five days, and he was not the preferred choice of President Lincoln or his general-in-chief, Henry W. Halleck. While Meade had the confidence of his former fellow corps commanders, there was no time for any major army reorganization. Meade would fight the battle with the Army of the Potomac much as he inherited it from his predecessor, Major General Joe Hooker. Lee, on the other hand, owing to the death of "Stonewall" Jackson, had just restructured his two-corps army into a three-corps army. And while Lee could certainly count on the reliability of his well-tested First Corp commander, Lieutenant General James Longstreet, he had some lingering concerns about his new II and III corps commanders, Lieutenant General Richard Ewell and Lieutenant General A. P. Hill respectively. As they came together, the two opposing armies were organized as so:

- A Union corps would consist of two or three divisions, with each division having two or three brigades apiece. The corps would have an artillery brigade of from five to eight batteries in support. If more than one corps was deployed, usually under a designated "wing commander," then additional artillery units from the Army of the Potomac's massive reserve artillery train could often be attached at the Army commander's discretion.
- A Confederate corps would consist of three divisions of from three to five brigades each, with each division having a battalion of about three to five artillery batteries. Each Confederate corps would also have a designated corps artillery reserve of usually two artillery battalions as support.
- The Army of the Potomac marched to Gettysburg with seven corps, while the Army of Northern Virginia invaded Pennsylvania with three corps. Both armies fielded a corps of cavalry, but only the Federals had an army-level artillery reserve. Once the Federal army was together, additional artillery batteries could be quickly dispatched from the artillery reserve as needed to tip the fight against the rebels. However, in the opening stages of a developing battle, until that artillery reserve arrived the Army of the Potomac would probably be fighting with overall artillery inferiority. Following the reserve artillery was a second artillery ammunition train, which gave the Army of Potomac a total of about 98,000 artillery rounds versus the approximately 44,000 carried by the Army of Northern Virginia. Hence the Union gunners never had to worry about artillery ammunition consumption, and consequently

each of their engaged guns would fire about 90 rounds per gun, while the Confederates had to be more conservative with their artillery and would only fire about 80 rounds per engaged gun.

As a comparison, here is how the armies roughly stacked up on June 30, 1863, the eve of the Battle of Gettysburg. In the summer of 1863, at least two corps from the Army of the Potomac were usually needed to match one corps from the Army of Northern Virginia. For various reasons, the actual number of troops engaged per corps would usually average about 1,000 to 2,000 fewer than shown below.

Army of the Potomac			
I Corps	Reynolds	3 divisions (7 infantry brigades), 1 artillery brigade	14,300 men, 28 guns
II Corps	Hancock	3 divisions (10 infantry brigades), 1 artillery brigade	13,500 men, 28 guns
III Corps	Sickles	2 divisions (6 infantry brigades), 1 artillery brigade	13,000 men, 30 guns
V Corps	Sykes	3 divisions (8 infantry brigades), 1 artillery brigade	13,200 men, 26 guns
VI Corps	Sedgwick	2 divisions (8 infantry brigades), 1 artillery brigade	15,700 men, 48 guns
XI Corps	Howard	3 divisions (6 infantry brigades), 1 artillery brigade	10,800 men, 26 guns
XII Corps	Slocum	2 divisions (6 infantry brigades), 1 artillery brigade	10,700 men, 20 guns
Artillery Reserve	Hunt/Tyler	5 artillery brigades	3,000 men, 114 guns
Cavalry Corps	Pleasanton	3 cavalry divisions (8 cavalry brigades), 2 horse artillery brigades	15,000 men, 52 guns

Army of Northern Virginia			
I Corps	Longstreet	3 divisions (11 infantry brigades), 5 artillery battalions	22,400 men, 87 guns
II Corps	Ewell	3 divisions (13 infantry brigades), 5 artillery battalions	21,800 men, 79 guns
III Corps	A. P. Hill	3 divisions (13 infantry brigades), 5 artillery battalions	23,300 men, 84 guns
Cavalry Division	Stuart	7 cavalry brigades, 2 horse artillery battalions	12,600 men, 33 guns

HISTORICAL LOSSES

Given the confusion in both armies following the July 1 fighting, the total losses for that one day are harder to document than the total casualties – killed, wounded and missing – for the entire battle. Consequently, the following numbers should be viewed only as a reasonable approximation of the results of the July 1 fighting.

- Union I Corps – Out of about 14,300 men, 12,200 were actually engaged with about 5,500 becoming casualties.
- Union XI Corps – Out of about 10,800 men, 9,400 were actually engaged with about 3,100 becoming casualties.
- Confederate II Corps – Out of about 21,800 men, 13,500 were actually engaged with about 3,200 becoming casualties.
- Confederate III Corps – Out of about 23,300 men, 14,000 were actually engaged with about 2,800 becoming casualties.

However, the casualties were not spread evenly across the engaged brigades, as some suffered a lot more than others. For instance, Scales' Brigade of Pender's division started its attack against Seminary Ridge with about 1,350 men, and that evening could muster only 500 effective soldiers, after somewhat less than an hour of combat. Meredith's Union "Iron Brigade" started the day with about 1,800 men and could only muster about 600 when it finally retreated to Culp's Hill. Individual regimental losses could vary even more. The 26th North Carolina Regiment of Pettigrew's Brigade suffered over 70 percent casualties in a prolonged point-blank fire fight with the 24th Michigan Regiment of Meredith's Brigade, which itself also suffered over 70 percent losses in that same engagement.

THE ARMY LISTS

Following is a list of all Union and Confederate units that were engaged or could have been engaged on the first day of Gettysburg. For the Army of the Potomac, this includes the I, III, XI, and XII Corps plus John Buford's cavalry division. For the Army of Northern Virginia, this includes all of its II and III Corps. If some individual regiments or brigades were not available due to temporary detached duty, that is also noted. Occasionally a one-time 1D6 die roll is used to determine availability at the beginning of the scenario and is so noted in the specific scenario instructions. In some cases, if it is a question of a variable time of arrival or release from the reserves, the gamer is usually given the option of rolling a 1D6 for that unit's possible arrival or release.

When units – regiments, brigades and even divisions – are noted as being "optional," that usually means that a deliberate command or administrative decision had been made that restricted or prevented their participation. However, had a different decision been made then that entire regiment, brigade or division could have been engaged. This was certainly the case of the Confederate divisions of Anderson (III Corps) and Johnson (II Corps), or the two divisions of Slocum's XII Corps. Divisions and brigades that are noted as optional should only be included with the mutual agreement of the players, as their inclusion could alter the balance of some of the scenarios. Nevertheless, these options give the military historian or interested civil war gamer the opportunity to explore the effect of alternative decisions that could have been made by the historical commanders.

ARMY OF THE POTOMAC – LEFT WING (I, III, XI & XII CORPS)

Left Wing Commander – Major General John Reynolds (2 LB)

Major General Oliver Otis Howard (1 LB) after Reynolds' death.

I CORPS – MAJOR GENERAL JOHN REYNOLDS (2 LB)
Major General Abner Doubleday (1 LB) after Reynolds' death.

I Corps/1st Division – Brigadier General James Wadsworth (1 LB)
1st Brigade – "The Iron Brigade" – Brigadier General Solomon Meredith (1 LB)
- 19th Indiana, 308 men, 6 figures, Rifle/Muskets, Elite
- 24th Michigan, 496 men, 8 figures, Rifle/Muskets, Veteran
- 2nd Wisconsin, 302 men, 6 figures, Mixed Muskets, Elite
- 6th Wisconsin, 344 men, 6 figures, Rifle/Muskets, Elite
- 7th Wisconsin, 364 men, 6 figures, Mixed Muskets, Elite

2nd Brigade – Brigadier General Lysander Cutler (1 LB)
- 76th New York, 375 men, 6 figures, Rifle/Musket, Veteran
- 84th New York, "14th Brooklyn", 318 men, 6 figures, Rifle/Musket, Elite
- 95th New York, 241 men, 4 figures, Rifle/Muskets, Elite
- 147th New York, 380 men, 6 figures, Rifle/Muskets, Veteran
- 56th Philadelphia, 252 men, 4 figures, Rifle/Muskets, Veteran
- *7th Indiana, 434 men, 8 figures, Rifle/Muskets, Veteran
  *Optional, on detached duty, availability determined by scenario.

I Corps/2nd Division – Brigadier General John Robinson (1 LB)
1st Brigade – Brigadier General Gabriel Paul (No LB)
Arrived near Seminary Ridge at about 12 noon on July 1.
- 13th Massachusetts, 284 men, 4 figures, Rifle/Muskets, Veteran
- 16th Maine, 298 men, 4 figures, Rifle/Muskets, Veteran
- 94th New York, 411 men, 6 figures, Rifle/Muskets, Veteran
- 104th New York, 285 men, 4 figures, Rifle/Muskets, Veteran
- 107th Philadelphia, 255 men, 4 figures, Rifle/Muskets, Veteran

2nd Brigade – Brigadier General Henry Baxter (1 LB)
Arrived near Seminary Ridge at about 12.30 p.m. on July 1.

- 12th Massachusetts, 261 men, 4 figures, Rifle/Muskets, Elite
- 83rd New York, 199 men, 4 figures, Rifle/Muskets, Elite
- 97th New York, 236 men, 4 figures, Rifle/Muskets, Veteran
- 11th Philadelphia, 270 men, 4 figures, Rifle/Muskets, Veteran
- 88th Philadelphia, 273 men, 4 figures, Rifle/Muskets, Veteran
- 90th Philadelphia, 208 men, 4 figures, Rifle/Muskets, Veteran

I Corps/3rd Division – Major General Abner Doubleday (1 LB)

Brigadier General Thomas Rowley (No LB) after Reynolds' death. This was a particularly unfortunate battlefield promotion for the Union, as General Rowley spent most of the day drunk wandering the battlefield and giving incoherent orders.

1st Brigade – Colonel Chapman Biddle (1 LB)
Arrived near Seminary Ridge at about 11.00 a.m. on July 1.

- 80th New York, 287 men, 4 figures, Rifle/Muskets, Veteran
- 121st Philadelphia, 263 men, 4 figures, Rifle/Muskets, Veteran
- 142nd Philadelphia, 336 men, 6 figures, Rifle/Muskets, Trained
- 151st Philadelphia, 467 men, 8 figures, Rifle/Muskets, Green

2nd Brigade – "The Second Pennsylvania Bucktails" – Colonel Roy Stone (1 LB)
Arrived near Seminary Ridge at about 10.30 a.m. on July 1.

- 43rd Philadelphia, 465 men, 8 figures, Rifle/Muskets, Trained
- 149th Philadelphia, 450 men, 8 figures, Sharpshooter-R/Muskets, Trained
- 150th Philadelphia, 400 men, 8 figures, Sharpshooter-R/Muskets, Trained

3rd Brigade – "The Paper Collar Brigade" – Brigadier General George Stannard (1 LB)
The 13th, 14th, and 16th Vermont would arrive by about 5 p.m., July 1 on Cemetery Ridge.

- 13th Vermont, 636 men, 10 figures, Rifle/Muskets, Trained
- 14th Vermont, 647 men, 10 figures, Rifle/Muskets, Trained
- 16th Vermont, 661 men, 10 figures, Rifle/Muskets, Trained
- *12th Vermont, 641 men, 10 figures, Rifle/Muskets, Trained
- *15th Vermont, 637 men, 10 figures, Rifle/Muskets, Trained

*Optional, on detached duty to guard I Corps trains, availability determined by scenario.

I Corps Artillery Brigade – Colonel Charles Wainwright (1 Arty LB)

- Hall's Battery (Maine Light, 2nd/B), three sections of 3" ordnance rifles, Elite
- Steven's Battery (Maine Light, 5th/E), three sections of Napoleons, Veteran
- Reynold's Battery (1st New York Light, L&E), three sections of 3" ordnance rifles, Veteran
- Cooper's Battery, (1st Philadelphia Light, B), two sections of 3" ordnance rifles, Veteran
- Stewart's Battery (4th US Regulars, B), three sections of Napoleons, Elite

III CORPS - MAJOR GENERAL DANIEL SICKLES (1 LB) (OPTIONAL)

III Corps was a victim of conflicting orders. Around noon, General Sickles had received General Reynolds' last message saying that "he had better come up." However, the army commander General Meade had previously ordered III Corps to stay put at Emmitsburg. General Sickles continued to dither until about 3 p.m. when he received General Howard's message that "General Reynolds is dead, for God's sake come up." At that point, General Sickles decided to respond, and after leaving two brigades and two batteries at Emmitsburg, he began moving the rest of III Corps up to Gettysburg. Ironically, that night Meade approved of Sickles' decision and then had him bring up the remaining two brigades and two batteries that had been left behind at Emmitsburg.

III Corps/1st Division, Major General David Birney (1 LB)

1st Brigade, Brigadier General Charles Graham (1 LB)
Historically, this unit would arrive at Cemetery Hill in the evening of July 1, 1863.

- 57th Philadelphia, 207 men, 4 figures, Rifle/Muskets, Veteran
- 63rd Philadelphia, 246 men, 4 figures, Rifle/Muskets, Veteran
- 68th Philadelphia, 320 men, 4 figures, Rifle/Muskets, Veteran
- 105th Philadelphia, 274 men, 4 figures, Rifle/Muskets, Veteran

- 114th Philadelphia, 259 men, 4 figures, Rifle/Muskets, Veteran
- 141st Philadelphia, 209 men, 4 figures, Rifle/Muskets, Veteran

2nd Brigade, Brigadier General Hobart Ward (1 LB)

Historically, this unit would arrive at Cemetery Hill in the evening of July 1, 1863.
- 20th Indiana, 400 men, 8 figures, Rifle/Muskets, Trained
- 3rd Maine, 210 men, 4 figures, Rifle/Muskets, Veteran
- 4th Maine, 287 men, 4 figures, Rifle/Muskets, Veteran
- 86th New York, 287 men, 4 figures, Rifle/Muskets, Veteran
- 124th New York, 238 men, 4 figures, Rifle/Muskets, Veteran
- 99th Philadelphia, 277 men, 4 figures, Rifle/Muskets, Veteran

United States Sharpshooters Brigade, Colonel Hiram Berdan (1 LB)

Administratively attached to Ward's Brigade but often operated as a divisional asset.
- *1st USS Sharpshooters, 240 men, 4 figures, Sharps B/L Rifles, Elite
- *2nd USS Sharpshooters, 240 men, 4 figures, Sharps B/L Rifles, Elite
  *See ADF Sharpshooter Rules

3rd Brigade, Colonel Philippe Regis de Trobriand (1 LB)

Historically, 3rd Brigade spent July 1 at Emmitsburg and would arrive in the vicinity of Cemetery Ridge on the morning of July 2, 1863.
- 17th Maine, 350 men, 6 figures, Rifle/Muskets, Veteran
- 3rd Michigan, 238 men, 4 figures, Rifle/Muskets, Elite
- 5th Michigan, 216 men, 4 figures, Rifle/Muskets, Elite
- *40th New York, 583 men, 10 figures, Rifle/Muskets, Trained
  *Includes 152 men of the 110th Philadelphia Regiment

III Corps/2nd Division, Brigadier General Andrew Humphreys (1 LB)

1st Brigade, Brigadier General Joseph Carr (1 LB)

Historically, 1st Brigade would arrive near Little Round Top on the evening of July 1, 1863.
- 1st Massachusetts, 321 men, 6 figures, Rifle/Muskets, Elite
- 11th Massachusetts, 286 men, 4 figures, Rifle/Muskets, Veteran
- 16th Massachusetts, 245 men, 4 figures, Rifle/Muskets, Veteran

- 12th New Hampshire, 224 men, 4 figures, Rifle/Muskets, Veteran
- 11th New Jersey, 275 men, 4 figures, Rifle/Muskets, Veteran
- 26th Philadelphia, 365 men, 6 figures, Rifle/Muskets, Veteran

2nd Brigade – "The Excelsior Brigade" – Colonel William Brewster (1 LB)

Historically, 2nd Brigade would arrive near Little Round Top on the evening of July 1.
- 70th New York, 288 men, 4 figures, Rifle/Muskets, Elite
- 71st New York, 243 men, 4 figures, Rifle/Muskets, Elite
- 72nd New York, 305 men, 6 figures, Rifle/Muskets, Veteran
- 73rd New York, 349 men, 6 figures, Rifle/Muskets, Veteran
- 74th New York, 266 men, 4 figures, Rifle/Muskets, Veteran
- 120th New York, 383 men, 6 figures, Rifle/Muskets, Veteran

3rd Brigade, Colonel George Burling (1 LB)

Historically, 3rd Brigade would spend July 1 at Emmitsburg and would re-join III Corps on the morning of July 2.
- 2nd New Hampshire, 354 men, 6 figures, Rifle/Muskets, Veteran
- 5th New Jersey, 206 men, 4 figures, Rifle/Muskets, Veteran
- 6th New Jersey, 207 men, 4 figures, Rifle/Muskets, Veteran
- 7th New Jersey, 275 men, 4 figures, Rifle/Muskets, Veteran
- *8th New Jersey, 321 men, 6 figures, Rifle/Muskets, Veteran
  *Includes 150 men from 115th Philadelphia

III Corps Artillery Brigade – Captain George Randolph (1 LB)

Judson's, Bucklyn's and Seely's batteries had arrived by the evening of July 1.
- Clark's Battery (1st New Jersey Light, 2nd/B), three sections of 10 pounder Parrott Rifles, Veteran
- Bucklyn's Battery (1st Rhode Island/E), three sections of Napoleons, Veteran
- Seely's Battery (4th US Regulars/K), three sections of Napoleons, Veteran
- * Winslow's Battery (1st New York/B), three sections of Napoleons, Veteran

- * Smith's Battery (4th NY Light), three sections of 10 pounder Parrott Rifles, Veteran
  * Historically, would spend July 1 at Emmitsburg and would re-join III Corps on the morning of July 2.

XI CORPS - MAJOR GENERAL OLIVER OTIS HOWARD (1 LB)
XI Corps/1st Division, Brigadier General Francis Barlow (1 LB)
1st Brigade – Colonel Leopold Von Gilsa (1 LB)
- 41st New York, 220 men, 4 figures, Rifle/Muskets, Veteran
- 68th New York, 230 men, 4 figures, Rifle/Muskets, Veteran
- 153rd Philadelphia, 500 men, 8 figures, Rifle/Muskets, Veteran
- 54th New York, 190 men, 4 figures, Rifle/Muskets, Veteran

2nd Brigade – Brigadier General Adelbert Ames (1 LB)
- 17th Connecticut, 390 men, 6 figures, Rifle/Muskets, Veteran
- 25th Ohio, 220 men, 4 figures, Rifle/Muskets, Veteran
- 75th Ohio, 270 men, 4 figures, Rifle/Muskets, Veteran
- 107th Ohio, 460 men, 8 figures, Rifle/Muskets, Trained

XI Corps/2nd Division, Brigadier General Adolph Von Steinwehr (1 LB)
1st Brigade – Colonel Charles Coster (1 LB)
- 134th New York, 400 men, 6 figures, Rifle/Muskets, Trained
- 154th New York, 240 men, 4 figures, Rifle/Muskets, Trained
- 27th Philadelphia, 280 men, 4 figures, Mixed Muskets, Veteran
- 73rd Philadelphia, 290 men, 4 figures, Rifle/Muskets, Veteran

2nd Brigade – Colonel Orlando Smith (1 LB)
  Not committed, held in reserve on Cemetery Hill.
- 33rd Massachusetts, 490 men, 8 figures, Rifle/Muskets, Veteran
- 136th New York, 480 men, 8 figures, Rifle/Muskets, Veteran
- 55th Ohio, 330 men, 6 figures, Rifle/Muskets, Veteran
- 73rd Ohio, 340 men, 6 figures, Rifle/Muskets, Veteran

XI Corps/3rd Division, Major General Carl Schurz (1 LB)
1st Brigade – Brigadier General Alexander Schimmelfennig (1 LB)
- 82nd Illinois, 320 men, 6 figures, Rifle/Muskets, Veteran
- 45th New York, 370 men, 6 figures, Rifle/Muskets, Veterans

- 157th New York, 410 men, 8 figures, Rifle/Muskets, Veteran
- 61st Ohio, 250 men, 4 figures, Rifle/Muskets, Elite
- 74th Philadelphia, 330 men, 6 figures, Rifle/Muskets, Veteran

2nd Brigade – Colonel Waldimir Krzyzanowski (1 LB)
- 58th New York, 190 men, 4 figures, Rifle/Muskets, Veteran
- 119th New York, 260 men, 4 figures, Rifle/Muskets, Veteran
- 82nd Ohio, 310 men, 6 figures, Rifle/Muskets, Veteran
- 75th Philadelphia, 210 men, 4 figures, Rifle/Muskets, Elite
- 26th Wisconsin, 450 men, 8 figures, Rifle/Muskets, Veteran

XI Corps Artillery Brigade – Major Thomas Osborne (1 LB)
- Wheeler's Battery (New York Light/13th Bat), two sections of 3" rifles, Veteran
- Dilger's Battery (1st Ohio Light/I), three sections of Napoleons, Elite
- Heckman's Battery (1st Ohio Light/K), two sections of Napoleons, Veteran
- Wilkeson's Battery (4th US/G), three sections of Napoleons, Veteran
- *Weidrich's Battery (1st New York Light/I), three sections of 3" ordnance rifles, Veteran
  *Not committed, was held in reserve on Cemetery Hill.

XII CORPS - MAJOR GENERAL HENRY SLOCUM (1 LB)
Despite pleas from General Howard at Gettysburg, General Slocum had decided to wait most of the afternoon at Two Taverns, just five miles away, before moving forward to Gettysburg, as he expected the army to retire to the Pipe Creek position. However, had he responded immediately and marched to the sound of the guns, his first division could have begun arriving as early as 2 p.m. or 3 p.m., though elements of his second division probably would still have been held in reserve or sent to guard the Round Tops as they actually were. This option is the basis for the two eastern board scenarios, "Slocum Arrives" and "If Slocum Wasn't Slow," which start at 2 or 3 p.m. respectively.

XII Corps/1st Division, Brigadier General Alpheus Williams (1 LB)
Historically Williams' division had just deployed to attack Wolf's Hill south of the Hanover Road by 6 p.m., but was recalled before the attack had started and re-joined Federal forces on the Baltimore Pike by about 7.30 p.m. By dark it was in reserve on Cemetery Hill.

1st Brigade, Colonel Archibald McDougall (1 LB)

- 5th Connecticut, 318 men, 6 figures, Rifle/Muskets, Veteran
- 20th Connecticut, 380 men, 6 figures, Rifle/Muskets, Veteran
- 3rd Massachusetts, 242 men, 4 figures, Rifle/Muskets, Elite
- 123rd New York, 472 men, 8 figures, Rifle/Muskets, Veteran
- 145th New York, 264 men, 4 figures, Rifle/Muskets, Veteran
- 46th Philadelphia, 296 men, 4 figures, Rifle/Muskets, Elite

2nd Brigade, Brigadier General Harry Lockwood (1 LB)

- 1st Maryland, Eastern Shore, 583 men, 10 figures, Rifle/Muskets, Trained
- 1/1st Maryland, Potomac Home Brigade, 370 men, 6 figures, Rifle/Muskets, Trained
- 2/1st Maryland, Potomac Home Brigade, 370 men, 6 figures, Rifle/Muskets, Trained
- 1/150th New York, 323 men, 6 figures, Rifle/Muskets, Trained
- 2/150th New York, 323 men, 6 figures, Rifle/Muskets, Trained

3rd Brigade, Brigadier General Thomas Ruger (1 LB)

- 27th Indiana, 339 men, 6 figures, Rifle/Muskets, Veteran
- 2nd Massachusetts, 397 men, 6 figures, Rifle/Muskets, Elite
- 13th New Jersey, 360 men, 6 figures, Rifle/Muskets, Veteran
- 107th New York, 346 men, 6 figures, Rifle/Muskets, Veteran
- 3rd Wisconsin, 285 men, 4 figures, Rifle/Muskets, Elite

XII Corps/2nd Division, Brigadier General John Geary (1 LB)

Historically, upon arriving at about 6 p.m. the whole division was sent to secure the Round Tops.

1st Brigade, Colonel Charles Candy (1 LB)

- 5th Ohio, 299 men, 4 figures, Rifle/Muskets, Elite
- 7th Ohio, 282 men, 4 figures, Rifle/Muskets, Elite
- 29th Ohio, 315 men, 6 figures, Rifle/Muskets, Veteran
- 66th Ohio, 299 men, 4 figures, Rifle/Muskets, Veteran
- 28th Philadelphia, 303 men, 6 figures, Rifle/Muskets, Veteran
- 147th Philadelphia, 298 men, 4 figures, Rifle/Muskets, Veteran

2nd Brigade, Brigadier General Thomas Kane (1 LB)

- 29th Philadelphia, 357 men, 6 figures, Rifle/Muskets, Veteran

- *111th Philadelphia, 340 men, 6 figures, Rifle/Muskets, Veteran
  *Includes 149 men from the 109th Philadelphia

3rd Brigade, Brigadier General George Greene (2 LB)

- 60th New York, 273 men, 4 figures, Rifle/Muskets, Veteran
- 78th New York, 198 men, 4 figures, Rifle/Muskets, Elite
- 102 New York, 230 men, 4 figures, Rifle/Muskets, Veteran
- 137 New York, 423 men, 8 figures, Rifle/Muskets, Veteran
- 149th New York, 297 men, 4 figures, Rifle/Muskets, Veteran

XII Corps Artillery Brigade – Lt Edward D. Muhlenberg (1 LB)

- Winegar's Battery (1st New York Light/B), two sections of 10 pounder Parrott Rifles, Veteran
- Atwell's Battery (Philadelphia Light/E), three sections of 10 pounder Parrott Rifles, Veteran
- Rugg's Battery (4th US Regulars/F), three sections of Napoleons, Veteran
- Kinzie's Battery (5th US Regulars/K), two sections of Napoleons, Veteran

ARMY OF THE POTOMAC - FIRST DIVISION - CAVALRY CORPS

Cavalry in *ADF* is modeled as one figure equals 30 men to reflect the larger space that cavalry would occupy. The cavalry of both sides, when used as a screening force, would usually deploy as battalions of two or more troops or companies each, and consequently the cavalry regiments in *ADF* are usually portrayed as two or three battalions per regiment, with each battalion usually functioning as an individual maneuver element when desired.

1st Cavalry Division – Brigadier General John Buford (2 LB)

From 2nd Brigade Horse Artillery – Assigned to 1st Cavalry Division

- Calef's Battery (2nd US Horse Artillery/A), three sections, 3 inch rifles, Elite

1st Cavalry Brigade – Colonel William Gamble (1 LB)

- 1/8th Illinois, 235 men, 8 figures, Sharps BL Carbines, Veteran
- 2/8th Illinois, 235 men, 8 figures, Sharps BL Carbines, Veteran
- 1/3rd Indiana, 156 men, 6 figures, BL Carbines, Elite
- 2/3rd Indiana, 156 men, 6 figures, BL Carbines, Elite
- 1/12th Illinois, 116 men, 4 figures, BL Carbines, Elite
- 1/12th Illinois, 116 men, 4 figures, BL Carbines, Elite

- 1/8th New York, 193 men, 6 figures, Veteran, Sharps BL Carbines, Elite
- 2/8th New York, 193 men, 6 figures, Veteran, Sharps BL Carbines, Veteran
- 3/8th New York, 193 men, 6 figures, Veteran, Sharps BL Carbines, Veteran

2nd Cavalry Brigade – Colonel Thomas Devin (1 LB)
- 1/9th New York, 183 men, 6 figures, Sharps BL Carbines, Veteran
- 2/9th New York, 183 men, 6 figures, Sharps BL Carbines, Veteran
- 1/17th Philadelphia, 232 men, 8 figures, BL Carbines, Veteran
- 2/17th Philadelphia Regiment, 232 men, 8 figures, BL Carbines, Veteran
- 1/6th New York, 135 men, 4 figures, Sharps BL Carbines, Elite
- *2/6th New York, 135 men, 4 figures, Sharps BL Carbines, Elite

    *Includes 63 men of the 3rd West Virginia

3rd Cavalry Brigade – Brigadier General Wesley Merritt (1 LB)

Merritt was held back to guard supply trains at Mechanicsburg, Maryland and then served as Cavalry Corps HQ Reserve. He would not see action until July 3, 1863.
- 1/6th Philadelphia, 121 men, 4 figures, Sharps BL Carbines, Veteran
- 2/6th Philadelphia, 121 men, 4 figures, Sharps BL Carbines, Veteran
- 1/1st US, 181 men, 6 figures, Sharps BL Carbines, Elite
- 2/1st US, 181 men, 6 figures, Sharps BL Carbines, Elite
- 1/2nd US, 203 men, 6 figures, Sharps BL Carbines, Elite
- 2/2nd US, 203 men, 6 figures, Sharps BL Carbines, Elite
- 1/5th US, 153 men, 4 figures, Sharps BL Carbines, Veteran
- 2/5th US, 153 men, 4 figures, Sharps BL Carbines, Veteran
- 1/6th US, 235 men, 6 figures, Sharps BL Carbines, Veteran
- 2/6th US, 235 men, 6 figures, Sharps BL Carbines, Veteran

ARMY OF NORTHERN VIRGINIA (II & III CORPS)

III CORPS
Lieutenant General Ambrose Powell Hill (1 LB)

III Corps/Heth's Division – Major General Henry Heth (1 LB)
Archer's Brigade – Brigadier General James Archer (1 LB)
- 1st Tennessee, 281 men, 4 figures, Rifle/Muskets, Elite
- 7th Tennessee, 249 men, 4 figures, Rifle/Muskets, Veteran

- 14th Tennessee, 220 men, 4 figures, Rifle/Muskets, Veteran
- *13th Alabama, 443 men, 8 figures, Rifle/Muskets, Veteran
    *Includes 135 men of the 5th Alabama Battalion

Davis' Brigade – Brigadier General Joseph Davis (No LB)
- 2nd Mississippi, 492 men, 8 figures, Rifle/Muskets, Veteran
- 42nd Mississippi, 575 men, 10 figures, Rifle/Musket, Trained
- 55th North Carolina, 640 men, 10 figures, Rifle/Musket, Trained
- *11th Mississippi, 592 men, 10 figures, Rifle/Musket, Trained

    * Detached duty guarding supply trains. Roll 1D6 for availability: a result of 1 or 2 means they are available.

Pettigrew's Brigade – Brigadier General James Pettigrew (1 LB)
- 11th North Carolina, 617 men, 10 figures, Rifle/Muskets, Trained
- 1/26th North Carolina, 418 men, 6 figures, Rifle/Muskets, Trained
- 2/26th North Carolina, 418 men, 6 figures, Rifle/Muskets, Trained
- 47th North Carolina, 567 men, 10 figures, Rifle/Muskets, Green
- 52nd North Carolina, 553 men, 10 figures, Rifle/Muskets, Green

Brockenbrough's Brigade – Colonel John Brockenbrough (1 LB)
- 40th Virginia, 254 men, 4 figures, Rifle/Muskets, Veteran
- 47th Virginia, 209 men, 4 figures, Rifle/Muskets, Veteran
- 55th Virginia, 268 men, 4 figures, Rifle/Muskets, Veteran
- 22nd Virginia, 237 men, 4 figures, Rifle/Muskets, Veteran

Heth's Divisional Artillery, Garnett's Battalion – Lieutenant Colonel John Garnett (No LB)

For reasons that remain unclear, on the morning of July 1 Garnett was relieved of duty by Lee's chief of artillery, Brigadier General William Pendleton, and consequently his battalion was never committed during the fighting as an entire battalion – on the first day only Maurin's battery saw serious action. However, at about 5 p.m. all of Garnett's batteries were released and were finally brought forward eventually to set up on Seminary Ridge.
- Grandy's Battery (Norfolk Light), two sections of mixed guns, Veteran
- Lewis' Battery (Pittsylvania Artillery), two sections of mixed guns, Veteran

- Maurin's Battery (Donaldsonville Artillery), two sections of 3" ordnance rifles, Veteran
- Moore's Battery (Virginia Artillery), two sections of mixed guns, Veteran

III Corps/Pender's Division – Major General William Dorsey Pender (1 LB)

Perrin's Brigade – Colonel Abner Perrin (1 LB)
- 1st South Carolina, 328 men, 6 figures, Smoothbore Muskets, Elite
- 12th South Carolina, 366 men, 6 figures, Rifle/Muskets, Veteran
- 13th South Carolina, 390 men, 6 figures, Rifle/Muskets, Veteran
- 14th South Carolina, 428 men, 8 figures, Rifle/Muskets, Veteran
- *1st South Carolina Rifles, 366 men, 6 figures, Rifle/Muskets, Elite
   * Detached duty guarding supply trains. Roll 1D6 for availability: a result of or 2 means they are available.

Lane's Brigade – Brigadier General James Lane (1 LB)
- 7th North Carolina, 291 men, 4 figures, Rifle/Muskets, Elite
- 18th North Carolina, 346 men, 6 figures, Rifle/Muskets, Veteran
- 28th North Carolina, 346 men, 6 figures, Rifle/Muskets, Veteran
- 33rd North Carolina, 368 men, 6 figures, Rifle/Muskets, Veteran
- 37th North Carolina, 379 men, 6 figures, Rifle/Muskets, Veteran

Scales' Brigade – Brigadier General Alfred Scales (1 LB)
- 13th North Carolina, 232 men, 4 figures, Rifle/Muskets, Veteran
- 16th North Carolina, 321 men, 6 figures, Rifle/Muskets, Veteran
- 2nd North Carolina, 267 men, 4 figures, Rifle/Muskets, Elite
- 34th North Carolina, 311 men, 6 figures, Rifle/Muskets, Veteran
- 38th North Carolina, 216 men, 4 figures, Smoothbore Muskets, Veteran

Thomas' Brigade – Brigadier General Edward Thomas (1 LB)
   Upon arriving on Herr Ridge, the III Corps commander, Lieutenant General A. P. Hill, decided to hold Thomas' brigade in reserve as support for the Confederate guns on Herr Ridge, and hence it saw no action that day. However, it was there and available, and depending on the scenario could be released for action.
- 14th Georgia, 305 men, 6 figures, Rifle/Muskets, Veteran
- 35th Georgia, 305 men, 6 figures, Rifle/Muskets, Veteran
- 45th Georgia, 305 men, 6 figures, Rifle/Muskets, Veteran
- 49th Georgia, 329 men, 6 figures, Rifle/Muskets, Veteran

Pender's Divisional Artillery Battalion – Major William Pogue (1 LB)
   Historically, although Pender's Division was ultimately committed to the attack, its divisional artillery was kept in reserve and saw no relevant action on July 1. However, towards the end of the battle at about 4.30 p.m. they were brought forward and eventually took up a position on Seminary Ridge facing Cemetery Hill.
- Wyatt's Battery (Albemarle Artillery), two sections of mixed guns, Veteran
- Graham's Battery (Charlotte Artillery), two sections of mixed guns, Veteran
- Ward's Battery (Madison Light Artillery), two sections of mixed guns, Veteran
- Brooke's Battery (Warrington Battery), two sections of mixed guns, Veteran

III Corps/Anderson's Division – Major General Richard Anderson (1 LB) Optional Unit
   On July 1, Anderson's Division had been delayed by the huge traffic jam on the Chambersburg Pike caused by Johnson's division interposing in front of it, and consequently the head of his column did not reach Herr Ridge until about 7 p.m. At that point, General Lee ordered Anderson to go into bivouac and serve as a reserve. However, had Johnson's division been ordered to proceed to Gettysburg down the Carlisle Pike – with the rest of its corps – rather than on to the Chambersburg Pike, then Anderson's Division could have started arriving at about 3 p.m. along the Chambersburg Pike and been deployed by about 4 p.m. behind Pender's Division. However, General Lee would probably still have held back at least one or two brigades and possibly Lane's Artillery Battalion as a reserve against the unexpected. This would have still have allowed most of Anderson's brigades to begin entering in battle formation at about 3.30 p.m. on the west edge of the battle space.

Wilcox's Brigade – Brigadier General Cadmus Wilcox (2 LB)
- 8th Alabama, 477 men, 8 figures, Rifle/Muskets, Veteran
- 9th Alabama, 306 men, 6 figures, Rifle/Muskets, Elite
- 10th Alabama, 311 men, 6 figures, Rifle/Muskets, Veteran
- 11th Alabama, 311 men, 6 figures, Rifle/Muskets, Veteran
- 14th Alabama, 316 men, 6 figures, Rifle/Muskets, Veteran

Mahone's Brigade – Brigadier General William Mahone (1 LB)
- 6th Virginia, 288 men, 4 figures, Rifle/Muskets, Elite
- 12th Virginia, 348 men, 6 figures, Rifle/Muskets, Veteran
- 16th Virginia, 270 men, 4 figures, Rifle/Muskets, Veteran
- 41st Virginia, 276 men, 4 figures, Rifle/Muskets, Veteran
- 61st Virginia, 356 men, 6 figures, Rifle/Muskets, Veteran

Lang's Brigade – Colonel David Lang (1 LB)
- 2nd Florida, 244 men, 4 figures, Rifle/Muskets, Elite
- 5th Florida, 248 men, 4 figures, Rifle/Muskets, Veteran
- 8th Florida, 248 men, 4 figures, Rifle/Muskets, Veteran

Wright's Brigade – Brigadier General Ambrose Wright (1 LB)
- 3rd Georgia, 441 men, 8 figures, Rifle/Muskets, Veteran
- 22nd Georgia, 400 men, 8 figures, Rifle/Muskets, Veteran
- *48th Georgia, 568 men, 10 figures, Rifle/Muskets, Trained
   *Includes 173 men of the 2nd Georgia Battalion

Posey's Brigade – Brigadier General Carnot Posey (1 LB)
- 12th Mississippi, 305 men, 6 figures, Rifle/Muskets, Veteran
- 16th Mississippi, 385 men, 6 figures, Rifle/Muskets, Veteran
- 19th Mississippi, 372 men, 6 figures, Rifle/Muskets, Veteran
- 48th Mississippi, 256 men, 4 figures, Rifle/Muskets, Veteran

Anderson's Divisional Artillery Battalion – Major John Lane (1 LB)
- Ross' Battery (Company A/Sumter Artillery), three sections of mixed guns, Veteran
- Patterson's Battery (Company B/Sumter Artillery), two sections of mixed guns, Veteran
- Wingfield's Battery (Company C/Sumter Artillery), three sections of mixed guns, Veteran

III Corps Artillery Reserve – Colonel Lindsay Walker (1 LB)

The III Corps Reserve Artillery, with Pegram in the lead, arrived early on Herr Ridge and provided valuable support for the fight for McPherson's Ridge. However, historically neither Pegram's nor McIntosh's battalions were brought forward for the attack on Seminary Ridge. Once Seminary Ridge was secured, both gun battalions were then brought forward to fire on Cemetery Hill.

Pegram's Artillery Battalion – Major William Pegram (1 Artillery LB)
- Johnson's Battery (Crenshaw Artillery), two sections of mixed guns, Veteran
- Marye's Battery (Fredericksburg Artillery), two sections of mixed guns, Veteran
- Bander's Battery (Letcher Artillery), two sections of mixed guns, Veteran
- Zimmerman's Battery (Pee Dee Artillery), two sections of 3" ordnance rifles, Veteran
- McGraw (Purcell Artillery), two sections of Napoleons, Veteran

McIntosh's Artillery Battalion – Major D. G. McIntosh (1 LB)
- Rice's Battery (Danville Artillery), two sections of Napoleons, Veteran
- Hurt's Battery (Hardaway Artillery), one section of 3" rifles, one section of Whitworth Rifles, Veteran
- Wallace's Battery (2nd Rockbridge Artillery), two sections of mixed guns, Veteran
- Johnson's Battery (Richmond Battery), two sections of 3" ordnance rifles, Veteran

II CORPS
Lieutenant General Richard Ewell (1 LB)

II Corps – Optional Attached Cavalry – Brigadier General Albert G. Jenkins (1 LB)

Jenkins' cavalry brigade was not well regarded in the Army of Northern Virginia. It was a loosely disciplined and erratically equipped group of irregular horsemen without any formal cavalry training. They were excellent marksmen, however, and when dismounted they fight as Veterans, but if mounted they fight as Green and any mounted charge is done in disorder. Due to administrative oversights, only the 17th Virginia would see action that first day, as dismounted support for General Jubal Early's divisional artillery battalion.

- 14th Virginia Cavalry, 265 men, 8 figures, Rifle/Muskets, Veteran/Green
- 16th Virginia Cavalry, 260 men, 8 figures, Rifle/Muskets, Veteran/Green
- 17th Virginia Cavalry, 241 men, 8 figures, Rifle/Muskets, Veteran/Green
- 34th Virginia Cavalry, 172 men, 6 figures, Rifle/Muskets, Veteran/Green
- 36th Virginia Cavalry, 107 men, 4 figures, Rifle/Muskets, Veteran/Green
- Jackson's Battery (Charlottesville Artillery) 2 sections of mixed guns, Veteran

II Corps/Rodes' Division, Major General Robert Rodes (1 LB)

- Blackford's Sharpshooters, 160-240 men, 4 figures, Sharpshooters R/M – Elite

Blackford's unit was administratively part of the 5th Alabama of O'Neal's Brigade, but Robert Rodes used them as a divisional asset to augment individual brigades depending on the mission. On the division's march down from Carlisle, they were with Iverson's Brigade as the division's advance guard. However, once the battle began they fought with Doles' Brigade against Barlow's Division.

Doles' Brigade – Brigadier General George Doles (2 LB)
- 4th Georgia, 340 men, 6 figures, Rifle/Muskets, Elite
- 12th Georgia, 330 men, 6 figures, Rifle/Muskets, Elite
- 44th Georgia, 360 men, 6 figures, Rifle/Muskets, Veteran
- 21st Georgia, 287 men, 4 figures, Rifle/Muskets, Elite

Daniel's Brigade – Brigadier General Junius Daniel (1 LB)
Optional deployment per specific scenario.
- 32nd North Carolina, 450 men, 8 figures, Rifle/Muskets, Veteran
- 43rd North Carolina, 570 men, 10 figures, Rifle/Muskets, Trained
- 45th North Carolina, 460 men, 8 figures, Rifle/Muskets, Trained
- 53rd North Carolina, 320 men, 6 figures, Rifle/Muskets, Trained
- 2nd North Carolina Battalion, 250 men, 4 figures, Rifle/Muskets, Veteran

Iverson's Brigade – Brigadier General Alfred Iverson (No LB)
- 5th North Carolina, 470 men, 8 figures, Rifle/Muskets, Veteran
- 12th North Carolina, 220 men, 4 figures, Rifle/Muskets, Veteran
- 20th North Carolina, 370 men, 6 figures, Rifle/Muskets, Veteran
- 23rd North Carolina, 210 men, 4 figures, Rifle/Muskets, Veteran

O'Neal's Brigade – Colonel Edward O'Neal (1 LB)
- 3rd Alabama, 350 men, 6 figures, Rifle/Muskets, Veteran
- 5th Alabama, 330 men, 6 figures, Rifle/Muskets, Veteran
- 6th Alabama, 380 men, 6 figures, Rifle/Muskets, Veteran
- 12th Alabama, 320 men, 6 figures, Rifle/Muskets, Veteran
- 26th Alabama, 320 men, 6 figures, Rifle/Muskets, Veteran

Ramseur's Brigade – Brigadier General Stephen Ramseur (1 LB)
- 2nd North Carolina, 240 men, 4 figures, Rifle/Muskets, Elite
- 4th North Carolina, 200 men, 4 figures, Rifle/Muskets, Elite
- 14th North Carolina, 300 men, 6 figures, Rifle/Muskets, Veteran
- 30th North Carolina, 280 men, 4 figures, Rifle/Muskets, Veteran

Rodes' Divisional Artillery Battalion – Lieutenant Colonel Thomas H. Carter (1 LB)
- Reese's Battery (Jeff Davis Artillery), 2 sections of 3" rifles, Veteran
- Carter's Battery (King Williams Artillery), 2 sections of mixed guns, Elite
- Page's Battery (Morris Virginia Artillery), 2 sections of Napoleons, Veteran
- Fry's Battery (Orange Virginia Artillery), 2 sections of 10 pounder Parrott Rifles, Veteran

II Corps/Early's Division, Major General Jubal Early (1 LB)
Gordon's Brigade – Brigadier General John Gordon (2 LB)
- 13th Georgia, 330 men, 6 figures, Rifle/Musket, Elite
- 31st Georgia, 269 men, 4 figures, Rifle/Musket, Elite
- 38th Georgia, 343 men, 6 figures, Rifle/Musket, Elite
- 60th Georgia, 318 men, 6 figures, Rifle/Musket, Veteran
- 61st Georgia, 307 men, 6 figures, Rifle/Musket, Veteran
- *26th Georgia, 333 men, 6 figures, Rifle/Musket, Elite

*Historically, the 26th GA was detailed to support Jones' artillery battalion. To reflect this, the 26th GA must stay adjacent to one of the artillery batteries until released. Roll 1D6 at the beginning of each Confederate turn for release, which takes a 1 or 2. In the actual battle the 26th GA was not released until the battle was almost over and the Union in full retreat.

Hays' Brigade – "The Louisiana Tigers" – Brigadier General Harry Hays (1 LB)
- 5th Louisiana, 209 men, 4 figures, Rifle/Muskets, Elite
- 6th Louisiana, 232 men, 4 figures, Rifle/Muskets, Elite
- 7th Louisiana, 248 men, 4 figures, Rifle/Muskets, Elite
- 8th Louisiana, 314 men, 6 figures, Rifle/Muskets, Veteran
- 9th Louisiana, 366 men, 6 figures, Rifle/Muskets, Veteran

Hoke's or Avery's Brigade – Colonel Isaac Avery (1 LB)
- 6th North Carolina, 533 men, 8 figures, Rifle/Muskets, Veteran
- 21st North Carolina, 454 men, 8 figures, Rifle/Muskets, Veteran
- 57th North Carolina, 316 men, 6 figures, Rifle/Muskets, Trained
- *54th North Carolina, 434 men, 8 figures, Rifle/Muskets, Trained
- *1st North Carolina Sharpshooters, 160 men, 4 figures, Sharpshooter Rifle/Muskets, Elite
  *Unlikely availability, roll 1D6 for each at start: a result of 1 or 2 means they are available.

Smith's Brigade – Brigadier General William Smith (No LB)
General "Extra Billy" Smith was a well-intentioned but easily confused commander. Sometime after 5 p.m. General Smith became convinced that a large Federal force was hovering off the Confederate right flank. He was so insistent that eventually General Early agreed to let his and Gordon's brigade redeploy off to the east to counter this threat. There was no Federal threat, but it did result in these two brigades being taken away from the battlefield at about 6 p.m.
- 1st Virginia, 280 men, 4 figures, Rifle/Muskets, Elite
- 49th Virginia, 280 men, 4 figures, Rifle/Muskets, Veteran
- 52nd Virginia, 271 men, 4 figures, Rifle/Muskets, Veteran

Early's Divisional Artillery Battalion – Lieutenant Colonel Hillary P. Jones (1 Artillery LB)
- Carrington's Battery (Charlottesville Artillery) – two sections of Napoleons, Elite
- Tanner's Battery (Courtney Virginia Artillery) – two sections of 3" ordnance rifles, Veteran
- Green's Battery (Louisiana Guard Artillery) – two sections of mixed guns, Veteran
- Garber's Battery (Staunton Virginia Artillery) – two sections of Napoleons, Veteran
- 17th Virginia Cavalry, 241 men, 8 figures, Rifle/Muskets, Veteran if dismounted/Green if mounted

II Corps/Johnson's Division, Major General Edward Johnson (1 LB)
Johnson's Division arrived sometime between 6 and 7 p.m. on the Chambersburg Pike and would proceed to march across the north of Gettysburg to reach the rest of II Corps, then northeast of Gettysburg. However, with better route planning it could have followed Rodes' Division down from Carlisle and arrived on the "North Edge" in battle formation as early as 4 p.m.

Steuart's Brigade – Brigadier General George Steuart (1 LB)
- 1st Maryland, 400 men, 8 figures, Rifle/Muskets, Veteran
- 1st North Carolina, 377 men, 6 figures, Rifle/Muskets, Elite
- 3rd North Carolina, 548 men, 10 figures, Rifle/Muskets, Trained
- 10th Virginia, 276 men, 4 figures, Rifle/Muskets, Elite
- 23rd Virginia, 251 men, 4 figures, Rifle/Muskets, Veteran
- 37th Virginia, 264 men, 4 figures, Rifle/Muskets, Veteran

Walker's Brigade – "The Stonewall Brigade" – Brigadier General James Walker (1 LB)
- 2nd Virginia, 333 men, 6 figures, Rifle/Muskets, Elite
- 4th Virginia, 257 men, 4 figures, Rifle/Muskets, Elite
- 5th Virginia, 345 men, 6 figures, Rifle/Muskets, Elite
- *33rd Virginia, 384 men, 6 figures, Rifle/Muskets, Elite
  *Includes 148 men from the 27th Virginia.

Williams' Brigade – "Nicholls' Louisiana Brigade" – Colonel Jesse Williams (1 LB)
- 10th Louisiana, 226 men, 4 figures, Rifle/Muskets, Veteran
- *2nd Louisiana, 408 men, 8 figures, Rifle/Muskets, Veteran
- **14th Louisiana, 461 men, 8 figures, Rifle/Muskets, Veteran
  *Includes 172 men from the 1st Louisiana.
  **Includes 186 men from the 15th Louisiana.

Jones' Brigade – Brigadier General John M. Jones (1 LB)
- 21st Virginia, 183 men, 4 figures, Rifle/Muskets, Elite
- 25th Virginia, 280 men, 6 figures, Rifle/Muskets, Elite
- 42nd Virginia, 252 men, 4 figures, Rifle/Muskets, Veteran
- 44th Virginia, 227 men, 4 figures, Rifle/Muskets, Veteran
- 48th Virginia, 252 men, 4 figures, Rifle/Muskets, Veteran
- 50th Virginia, 252 men, 4 figures, Rifle/Muskets, Veteran

Johnson's Divisional Artillery Battalion – Major Joseph Latimer (1 Artillery LB)
- Dement's Battery (1st Maryland Battery), two sections of Napoleons, Veteran
- Carpenter's Battery (Alleghany Artillery), two sections of mixed guns, Veteran

- Brown's Battery (Chesapeake Artillery), two sections of Napoleons, Veteran
- *1/Raine's Battery (1/Lee Virginia Artillery), one section of 10 pounder Parrott Rifles, Veteran
- *2/Raine's Battery (2/Lee Virginia Artillery), one section of 20 pounder Parrott Rifles, Veteran

  * Treat as two sections of 20 pounder Parrott Rifles for game purposes.

II Corps Artillery Reserve – Colonel J. Thompson Brown (1 LB)

The II Corps reserve artillery had also been sent along with Johnson's Division to re-join the Army advancing along the Chambersburg Pike, so Dance's and Nelson's artillery battalions would also contribute to the huge traffic jam at the Cashtown Gap.

Dance's Virginia Artillery Battalion – Captain Willis J. Dance (1 LB)

- Watson's Battery (2nd Richmond Howitzers), two sections of 10 pounder Parrott Rifles, Veteran
- Smith's Battery (3rd Richmond Howitzers), two sections of 3"ordnance rifles, Veteran
- Cunningham's Battery (Powhatan Artillery), two sections of 3" ordnance rifles, Veteran
- Graham's Battery (Rockbridge Artillery), two sections of 20 pounder Parrott Rifles, Elite
- Griffen's Battery (Salem Artillery), two sections of mixed guns, Veteran

Nelsen's Artillery Battalion – Lieutenant Colonel William Nelsen (1 LB)

- Kirkpatrick's Battery (Amherst Virginia Artillery), two sections of mixed guns, Veteran
- Massies' Battery (Fluvanna Virginia Artillery), two sections of mixed guns, Veteran
- Milledge's Battery (The Georgia Battery), two sections of mixed guns, Veteran

The Rebels swarm over Seminary Hill (Patrick LeBeau)

THE FIRST DAY OF GETTYSBURG – MUSTER POINT VALUES

For those gamers that prefer to create a balanced collision of forces while still reflecting the nature of the two armies of Gettysburg, the ADF Muster Point (MP) values of each brigade, division and corps are presented for the first day of Gettysburg as part of the Army Lists for this scenario set. It is recommended, however, that the gamers preserve the actual historical regiments within the brigades and then freely structure their "Summer of 1863" using the various brigades, divisions or corps with the overall organizational guidelines as previously discussed. Do note that cavalry brigades have a much higher point value than infantry brigades. This has been done to reflect the historically higher expense and longer time it takes to raise, train and maintain a cavalry unit as opposed to an infantry unit.

Even if a leader has no LBs he still costs the same Muster Points (MPs) as a 1 LB brigade or division commander since he does occupy the position. That said, even a no LB leader has an equivalent value of 1 for determining command and control distances.

With that in mind, a fairly balanced "Gettysburg Summer" battle could be had using a 650 to 750 point Army of Northern Virginia corps against two Army of the Potomac Union corps of about 250 to 350 points each. However, start the battle with the entire Confederate Corps deployed against just one of the Union Corps. Then have the second Union Corps coming on to the board just as the game starts or slightly later based on a die roll. At any time, an additional Union corps or a battalion or two of artillery from the Army of the Potomac's massive artillery reserve could certainly arrive. For further details on the use of how the ADF muster point system can be used to create scenarios, consult the original rules.

ARMY OF THE POTOMAC: I, III, XI, AND XII CORPS MUSTER POINT VALUES

The I Corps with Major General John Reynolds (321 MPs)	
I Corps – 1st Division with Brigadier General James Wadsworth (101 MPs)	Meredith's Brigade (43 MPs) Cutler's Brigade (50 MPs)
I Corps – 2nd Division with Brigadier General John Robinson (81 MPs)	Paul's Brigade (33 MPs) Baxter's Brigade (40 MPs)
I Corps – 3rd Division with Major General Abner Doubleday (123 MPs)	Biddle's Brigade (29 MPs) Stone's Brigade (30 MPs) Stannard's Brigade (56 MPs)
I Corps – Artillery Brigade with five batteries (55 MPs)	

The III Corps with Major General Daniel Sickles (342 MPs)	
III Corps – 1st Division with Major General David Birney (152 MPs)	Graham's Brigade (36 MPs) Ward's Brigade (39 MPs) Berdan's USS Brigade (32 MPs) Regis de Trobriand's Brigade (37 MPs)
III Corps – 2nd Division with Brigadier General Andrew Humphreys (131 MPs)	Carr's Brigade (42 MPs) Brewster's Brigade (46 MPs) Burling's Brigade (35 MPs)
III Corps – Artillery Brigade with five batteries (51 MPs)	

The XI Corps with Major General Oliver Otis Howard (287 MPs)	
XI Corps – 1st Division with Brigadier General Francis Barlow (69 MPs)	Leopold von Gilsa's Brigade (30 MPs) Ames' Brigade (31 MPs)
XI Corps – 2nd Division with Brigadier General Adolph von Steinwehr (70 MPs)	Coster's Brigade (24 MPs) Smith's Brigade (38 MPs)
XI Corps – 3rd Division with Major General Carl Schurz (90 MP)	Schimmelfenning's Brigade (43 MPs) Krzyzanowski's Brigade (39s)
XI Corps – Artillery Brigade with five batteries (50 MPs)	

The XII Corps with Major General Henry Slocum (295 MPs)	
XII Corps – 1st Division with Brigadier General Alpheus Williams (139 MPs)	McDougall's Brigade (48 MPs) Lockwood's Brigade (40 MPs) Ruger's Brigade (43s)
XII Corps – 2nd Division with Brigadier General John Geary (110 MPs)	Candy's Brigade (39 MPs) Kane's Brigade (20 MPs) Greene's Brigade (43 MPs)
XII Corps – Artillery Brigade with four batteries (38 MPs)	
1st Cavalry Division with Brigadier General John Buford (404 MPs)	Gamble's Brigade (138 MPs) Devin's Brigade (92 MPs) Merritt's Brigade (146 MPs) Calef's Horse Artillery Battery (12 MPs)

ARMY OF NORTHERN VIRGINIA: III AND II CORPS MUSTER POINT VALUES

III Corps with Lieutenant General Ambrose Powell Hill (648 MPs)	
III Corps – Heth's Division with Major General Henry Heth (168 MPs)	Archer's Brigade (32 MPs) Davis' Brigade (39 MPs) Pettigrew's Brigade (46 MPs) Brockenbrough's Brigade (26 MPs) Garnett's Divisional Artillery Battalion with four batteries (25 MPs)
III Corps – Pender's Division with Major General William Dorsey Pender (189 MPs)	Perrin's Brigade (46 MPs) Lane's Brigade (35 MPs) Scales' Brigade (36 MPs) Thomas' Brigade (34 MPs) Pogue's Divisional Artillery Battalion with four batteries (30 MPs)
III Corps – Anderson's Division with Major General Richard Anderson (213 MPs)	Wilcox's Brigade (51 MPs) Mahone's Brigade (37 MPs) Lang's Brigade (23 MPs) Wright's Brigade (34 MPs) Posey's Brigade (32 MPs) Lane's Divisional Artillery Battalion with three batteries (28 MPs)
III Corps – Reserve Artillery Brigade with Colonel L. Walker (70 MPs)	Pegram's Artillery Battalion with five batteries (38 MPs) McIntosh's Artillery Battalion with four batteries (26 MPs)

II Corps with Lieutenant General Richard Ewell (781 MPs)	
II Corps – Jenkins' Cavalry Brigade (60 MPs)	
II Corps – Rodes' Division with Major General Robert Rodes (242 MPs)	Blackford's Sharpshooters (11 MPs) Doles' Brigade (44 MPs) Daniel's Brigade (44 MPs) Iverson's Brigade (26 MPs) O'Neal's Brigade (41 MPs) Ramseur's Brigade (32 MPs) Carter's Divisional Artillery Battalion with four batteries (36 MPs)
II Corps – Early's Division with Major General Jubal Early (192 MPs)	Gordon's Brigade (60 MPs) Hay's Brigade (41 MPs) Hokes' or Avery's Brigade (38 MPs) Smith's Brigade (23 MPs) Jones' Divisional Artillery Battalion with four batteries (30 MPs)
II Corps – Johnson's Divisions with Major General Edward Johnson (204 MPs)	Steuart's Brigade (51 MPs) Walker's Brigade (38 MPs) Williams' Brigade (29 MPs) Jones' Brigade (42 MPs) Latimer's Divisional Artillery Battalion with four batteries (39 MPs)
II Corps – Reserve Artillery Battalion with Colonel J. Thompson Brown (75 MPs)	Dance's Artillery Battalion with five batteries (45 MPs) Nelsen's Artillery Battalion with three batteries (24 MPs)

REGIMENTS AND FRONTAGES

American Civil War enthusiasts have been debating frontages for many decades, and the answer that would be correct most of the time would be "whatever space they need to occupy for the mission at hand." By dropping companies into reserve a regiment could compress, or by going into a single line the regiment could extend. However, how long would a "text book" double-rank battle line actually be? In a post-war experiment, Cadet Captain B. Allison Colona of the Virginia Military Institute, using the VMI cadets, formed up regulation battle lines from 10 men to 1,000 men, measured how long each was and recorded those distances along with his detailed survey of the New Market battlefield. His actual notes are reproduced here. Being a senior engineering student, Cadet Captain Colona noted how long these lines would be in a precise map scale of 4 inches to one mile. However, once the command of "fire at will" was given, all those neat double lines would almost always disintegrate into a ragged scramble of men simply trying to load and fire as fast as they could.

SCALE OF FRONTS.
MEN IN TWO RANKS

No of Men	Fronts in feet	On Sc. 4"=1mi	Graphic Fronts
10	15	0.01	
50	75	0.06	
100	150	0.11	
200	300	0.23	
300	450	0.34	
400	600	0.46	
500	750	0.57	
600	900	0.68	
700	1050	0.80	
800	1200	0.91	
900	1350	1.02	
1000	1500	1.14	

THE DEVIL TO PAY

8 a.m.–11 a.m., July 1, 1863 – Northwest of Gettysburg

THE UNION SITUATION

"They will attack you in the morning and they will come booming with skirmishers three deep. You will have to fight like the devil to hold your own until support arrives." – Brigadier General John Buford, Commander, 1st Cavalry Division

General Buford's premonition that it would be a tough morning for his two brigades turned out to be all too true. At about 7 a.m. on a drizzly Wednesday morning along the Chambersburg Pike, pickets from the 8th Illinois cavalry of Gamble's Brigade exchanged shots with skirmishers of the 13th Alabama, and the Battle of

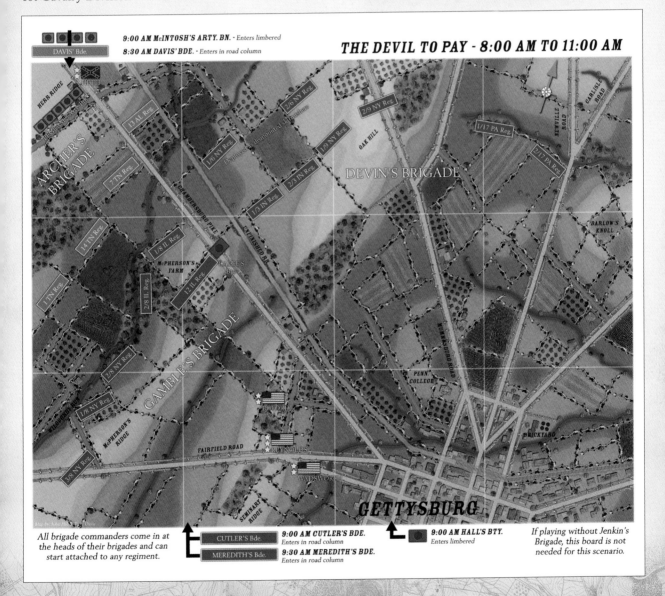

All brigade commanders come in at the heads of their brigades and can start attached to any regiment.

9:00 AM McINTOSH'S ARTY. BN. - *Enters limbered*
8:30 AM DAVIS' BDE. - *Enters in road column*

THE DEVIL TO PAY - 8:00 AM TO 11:00 AM

CUTLER'S Bde. — 9:00 AM CUTLER'S BDE. *Enters in road column*
MEREDITH'S Bde. — 9:30 AM MEREDITH'S BDE. *Enters in road column*

9:00 AM HALL'S BTY. *Enters limbered*

If playing without Jenkin's Brigade, this board is not needed for this scenario.

Outside the McPherson farm, Gamble's troopers continue to contest Archer's advancing skirmishers. (Figures: Cory Ring, photo: Chris Ward)

THE CONFEDERATE SITUATION

"Archer and Davis were now directed to advance, the object being to feel the enemy and to make a forced reconnaissance." – Major General Henry Heth

It had been a confusing day for General Heth. Without cavalry to screen his division, he had led with Pegram's artillery battalion and Archer's skirmishers, and they had proved useful in pushing back the initial Union cavalry screen he had encountered. He then deployed additional skirmishers from Archer's infantry brigade at his leisure and continued brushing the cavalry back, but their resistance had stiffened as the cavalry fell back from each succeeding ridge, one line covering the other. As he rode on to Herr Ridge, Heth noted that Pegram's Battalion had deployed all of his guns and so he ordered up Davis' brigade to the left of the Chambersburg Pike. If these pesky horsemen wanted a real fight he would give it to them: after all, it was only cavalry. Heth's commander, Lieutenant General A. P. Hill, had made it clear the night before that he "had no objection in the world" if Heth wanted to march his division into Gettysburg to get "some shoes."

SCENARIO SPECIFIC RULES

SCENARIO SETUP

The units set up as shown. The Confederate infantry, since they have been fighting cavalry, must set up in extended line or as skirmishers. The Union cavalry deploys in a cavalry line or as skirmishers. The indicated set up shows the maximum forward position of the participating units. However, any unit may either set up as indicated or up to two inches further back.

SCENARIO LENGTH

This scenario is six turns long, starting at with the 8 a.m. turn and ending with the 11 a.m. turn.

VICTORY CONDITIONS

For the Confederates to win, they must clear all Union units off either the north or the south side of McPherson's Ridge by the end of the 11 a.m. turn. McPherson's Ridge is divided into a north or south side by the railroad cut.

GAME INITIATIVE

As long as Major General Reynolds is alive, the Union has the initiative and can choose which side is active first in any one particular turn. If Reynolds is killed, then on all the following turns the initiative is

Gettysburg had begun. Gradually falling back from ridge to ridge, the Union horsemen inflicted almost no losses on the advancing Confederates, but they did force Archer's Brigade to deploy from road march into extended lines, which slowed the Rebel advance. Meanwhile to the north, pickets of the 17th Pennsylvania reported a predawn brush with some unidentified Rebel cavalry, but as nothing came of it Buford decided to bring Devin's entire brigade over to contest the growing Confederate strength that was coming down the Pike. As Buford's troopers retreated, they strengthened their line with Calef's horse artillery, which in turn prompted the Confederates to deploy additional forces, including Pegram's superb artillery battalion. Finally, just east of Willoughby Run on McPherson's Ridge, Buford's two cavalry brigades stopped retreating, as this would be their final stand. By mid-morning, it had already been a long and tough morning for his troopers, and when John Buford was joined by Major General John Reynolds in the cupola of the Lutheran seminary, Buford admitted that they indeed had "the devil to pay." From his vintage point in the cupola, John Buford could see the dust rising from the advancing columns of the Army of the Potomac's formidable I Corps moving up to relieve his cavalrymen. But would they get here in time?

determined by competitive 1D6 die roll, with a tie going to the Confederates.

CONFEDERATE INFANTRY

Archer's Brigade of Heth's Division has been skirmishing with Buford's cavalry since early morning and hence it does not have an opening volley benefit. Each brigade commander starts or enters the scenario attached to any one of his regiments. General Heth starts on Herr Ridge. Corps commander General A. P. Hill enters on Herr Ridge on the 10 a.m. turn.

UNION CAVALRY

All Union cavalry starts dismounted. The 17th Philadelphia starts behind the stream and cannot advance beyond it. By this time Buford's cavalry brigades and Calef's horse artillery battery were exhausted and beginning to run low on ammunition. To reflect this, they have a +1 MMP additional modifier to all morale checks and an additional -1 DRM to all their fires until the start of the 10 a.m. turn, when these penalties increase to +2 MMP for morale and -2 DRM for firing. These modifiers are over and above the "two worst" modifier restriction. Also, since the cavalry has been skirmishing all morning, it does not get any opening volley benefits. Beginning with the start of the 10 a.m. turn, every Union cavalry battalion and Calef's horse artillery battery must roll a 1D6 for immediate withdrawal as the Union infantry comes on to the battlefield. It takes a 5 or 6 for the cavalry units or Calef's battery to withdraw. When the unit withdraws, it is simply removed from the scenario (*Exception: In the expanded scenario, they might go into a "reserve"*). However, since it is considered to be a voluntary withdrawal, there is no morale detriment for element removed on the rest of the brigade. It is assumed that the brigade commanders, Colonels William Gamble and Thomas Devin, will stay on the board until their last unit withdraws and that the cavalry division commander also does so. The division commander, General John Buford, will remain until all the cavalry units have departed, at which time he will also depart.

HALL'S BATTERY

As Calef's horse artillery was getting ready to withdraw, Hall's battery of six ordnance rifles quickly dashed to the top of McPherson's Ridge and unlimbered before the Confederate artillery could react to its arrival. To reflect this, assume that when Hall first unlimbers any fire against him has neither the limbered artillery penalty nor the unlimbered artillery benefit. It is a straight even fire. If Hall's and Calef's battery do a combined fire, the -1

DRM for Calef being low on ammunition still applies to the combined fire.

OPTIONAL UNIT - JENKIN'S CAVALRY BRIGADE

"They would fight like veterans when they pleased, but had no idea of letting their own sweet wills be controlled by any orders, emanating from anyone." – General Bradley Johnston

One of the more quirky Confederate cavalry units was Jenkin's Brigade of Virginia mountain men. They were excellent woodsmen and marksmen, but since they had no formal training as a mounted force, they were more akin to irregular mounted infantry than regular cavalry. They did not take well to regular army discipline, protocols, or logistics. Jeb Stuart commented that they fought well on the third day until they ran out of ammunition as they had only brought ten rounds per man and when they ran out of ammunition, they left. Their mission was to gather supplies and create confusion, at which they were very good, and to provide a continuous cavalry screen for Ewell's corps, at which they were not so good. It appears that it probably was Ewell's intent to have Jenkins screen Rodes' advance down from Carlisle, but the orders were never issued or the courier could not find Jenkins. However, had the right orders and courier

Map by: John Hill & Todd Davis

Early in the morning Gamble's cavalry brigade with Calef's battery pass through Gettysburg on their way to meet the Confederates on the ridges west of the town. (Malcom Johnston)

connections have been made, then Jenkin's Brigade of mountain misfits might have been yet another issue that Buford's cavalry would have to deal with on the morning of July 1, 1863. Jenkin's Brigade can be included – or not – in any of the scenarios that use the middle board, as their most probable mission would have been screening for Rodes' Division moving down from Carlisle. (See the following special rules for Jenkins' Brigade).

UNION CAVALRY RESERVE

For Union cavalry withdrawal, if a 6 is rolled, the unit is spent and it withdraws out of the scenario. However, if a 5 is rolled the unit retires to Gettysburg as a reserve. Starting with its next active turn, it can be used anywhere on the center Gettysburg town board.

JENKINS' CAVALRY BRIGADE – ENTRY RULES

At the start of each Confederate active turn, roll a 1D6. If a 1 or 2 is rolled, Jenkins' Brigade enters as shown. The 34th Virginia Cavalry and the 36th Virginia Cavalry enter as dismounted skirmishers and move up to the fence as shown with their first action; they have one action left. The 14th Virginia and 16th Virginia enter dismounted. They and Jackson's Battery have only one action and they must use it to enter as shown.

JENKINS' BRIGADE – COMBAT RULES

Jenkins' Brigade fights as Veteran when dismounted and Green when mounted. Any unit of Jenkins' Brigade must pass a mounted morale check before making any mounted charge, and any mounted charge made is done in disorder. However, they were very good marksmen and they get a +1 DRM for any fires, in addition to any other firing benefits, but any firing where they roll all 5s or 6s runs them out of ammunition and that unit retires off the field and is gone.

HISTORICAL OUTCOME

Historically, the Federals won this scenario and the two involved brigades of Generals Archer and Davis were severely punished, with Davis becoming the first Confederate general to have been taken prisoner. However, a strong case can be made that the heavy damage inflicted on those two Confederate brigades was not worth the loss of General Reynolds, as his death may have been a significant factor in the ultimate Union defeat on the first day. This battle would be the start of a very long hard day for Cutler and Meredith's "Iron Brigade," as it will be fighting in all of the Chambersburg Pike scenarios. By the time it was over, a very tired and blooded "Iron Brigade" trudged to its final position on Culp's Hill south of Gettysburg, having been whittled down to about 600 effectives out of the 1,800 it had started with.

Though Buford's two cavalry brigades were pulled out as the I Corps infantry arrived, their day was not yet over. Gamble's brigade took up a position at the end of final Union line on Seminary Ridge where the 8th Illinois drew sabers and made a mounted advance – feigning a charge – against Lane's Confederate brigade. Fearful of a mounted charge by Gamble's horsemen, two of Lane's

Buford's cavalry hold Heth's advance, by Adam Hook © Osprey Publishing Ltd. Taken from Campaign 52: Gettysburg 1863.

regiments appeared to have stopped and formed square. Meanwhile, Devin's cavalry brigade was sent to screen the northeast approaches to Gettysburg, where it detected and harassed the approach of Early's Division of Ewell's II Corps.

SUMMARY ORDER OF BATTLE

(For brigade, regiment and battery details see Army List)

THE UNION FORCES

Left Wing/I Corps, Major General Thomas Reynolds (2 LB)

1st Cavalry Division, Brigadier General John Buford (2 LB)
- Gamble's – 1st Brigade – Colonel William Gamble (1 LB)
- Devin's – 2nd Brigade – Colonel Thomas Devin (1 LB)
- 2nd Brigade Horse Artillery, Calef's Battery

I Corps/1st Division, Brigadier General James Wadsworth (1 LB)
- Meredith's – 1st Brigade, Brigadier General Solomon Meredith (1 LB) (9.30 a.m.)
- Cutler's – 2nd Brigade, Brigadier General Lysander Cutler (1 LB) (arrives 9 a.m.)
- From I Corps Artillery Brigade: Hall's Battery

THE CONFEDERATE FORCES

III Corps/Heth's Division, Major General Henry Heth (No LB)
- Archer's Brigade – Brigadier General James Archer (1 LB) (9 a.m.)
- Davis' Brigade – Brigadier General Joseph Davis (no LB)

III Corps Reserve Artillery
Pegram's Artillery Battalion – Major William Pegram (+1 Artillery LB)
- Johnson's Battery
- Marye's Battery
- Bander's Battery
- Zimmerman's Battery
- McGraw's Battery

McIntosh's Artillery Battalion – Major D. G. McIntosh (1 LB)
- Rice's Battery
- Hurt's Battery
- Wallace's Battery
- Johnson's Battery

Optional – Jenkin's Cavalry Brigade of Ewell's Corps (see Scenario Specific Rules).

MCPHERSON'S RIDGE

2 p.m.–4 p.m., July 1, 1863 – Northwest of Gettysburg

THE CONFEDERATE SITUATION

"I am in ignorance of as to what we have in front of us here. It may be the whole Federal Army, or it may only be a detachment. If it is the whole Federal force, we must fight a battle here." – General Robert E. Lee

It had not been a particularly good morning for General Robert E. Lee, and an even worse one for Henry Heth's Division of the III Corps of the Army of Northern Virginia. All morning, Lee had been expecting to hear from his cavalry commander, Major General J. E. B. Stuart, as to the location and strength of the main body of the Army of the Potomac. He could hear from the distant booming of Pegram's and McIntosh's artillery battalions that the advance elements of his army were probably in contact with something more than Pennsylvania militia or a protecting cavalry screen. Riding forward, he met up with his III Corps commander, Lieutenant General A. P. Hill, who informed Lee that Henry Heth's division had been engaged that morning and that its two lead brigades had suffered a serious repulse.

Continuing to ride forward at about 1.30 p.m., Lee and Hill were met by a frustrated and anxious General Henry Heth who confirmed that his two leading brigades under brigadier generals Davis and Archer had indeed been roughly handled and that General Archer himself had been taken prisoner. Desiring to redeem his situation, Henry pleaded for permission for a general attack, to which Lee responded, "No, I am not prepared to bring on a general engagement today – Longstreet is not up." Nevertheless, Lee continued to watch the situation develop and sometime after 2 p.m., following yet another request from General Heth, Lee finally agreed that Heth's division could launch a general attack and that Major General William Dorsey Pender's division would be brought up in support if needed. Shortly after 2 p.m., Heth's division was moving forward to attack and Pender's division was forming as a reserve. This is where the fighting became much more serious.

The Union resets its defense on McPherson's Ridge as Heth regroups below. (Patrick LeBeau & Chris Ward)

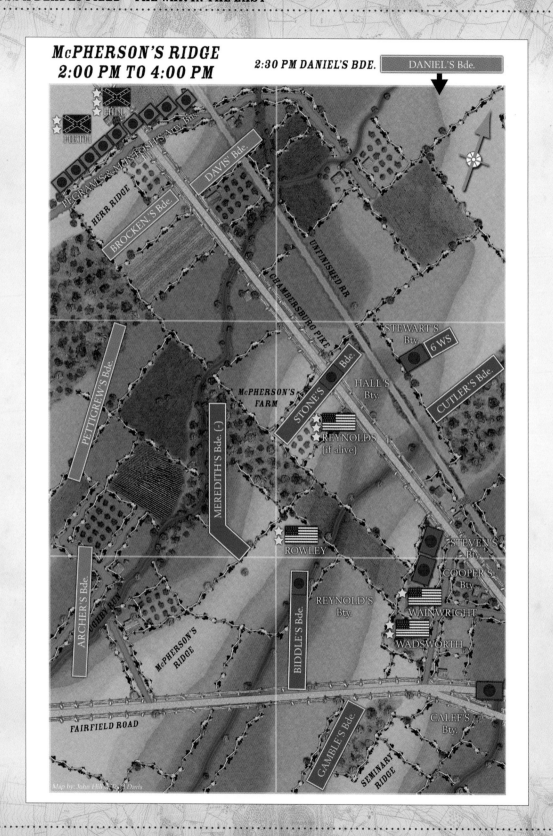

McPHERSON'S RIDGE
2:00 PM TO 4:00 PM

2:30 PM DANIEL'S BDE.

DANIEL'S Bde.

A.P. HILL

HETH

PEGRAM'S & McINTOSH'S Arty. Bns.

HERR RIDGE

BROCKEN'S Bde.

DAVIS Bde.

UNFINISHED RR

CHAMBERSBURG PIKE

STEWART'S Bty.

6 WS

CUTLER'S Bde.

McPHERSON'S FARM

STONE'S Bde.

HALL'S Bty.

PETTIGREW'S Bde.

MEREDITH'S Bde. (-)

REYNOLDS
(if alive)

ROWLEY

STEVEN'S Bty.

COOPER'S Bty.

WAINWRIGHT

WADSWORTH

ARCHER'S Bde.

WILLOUGHBY RUN

McPHERSON'S RIDGE

BIDDLE'S Bde.

REYNOLD'S Bty.

FAIRFIELD ROAD

GAMBLE'S Bde.

CALEF'S Bty.

SEMINARY RIDGE

Map by: John Hill & Todd Davis

THE UNION SITUATION

"I saw the enemy slowly approaching up the hill, extending far beyond our left flank, for which we had no defense." – Major Alexander Biddle, 121st Pennsylvania

On the surface, it had not been a bad morning for the Federals. The arrival of the Union I Corps had definitely surprised the Confederates and Meredith's and Cutler's Brigades had seriously mauled Heth's advance brigades. The arrival of Biddle's and Stone's brigades were certainly welcome, as was the rest of the I Corps artillery. The rebuilding of the Union defense was made possible by the Confederate gift of time, as between 12 noon and 2 p.m. the rebels had refrained from any serious attacks. However, it was obvious that was about to change as Heth's entire division advanced off Herr Ridge.

As good as the morning's fighting had been, it could not make up for the death of General Reynolds. His guiding hand and instinctive grasp of a battlefield situation was sorely missed. Critical redeployments had not been made and Meredith's "Iron Brigade" flanks were both unsupported. Reynold's death had changed the entire dynamics of the first day's battle, as it propelled a whole host of people into positions that were probably beyond their capability. The most significant shift was that the senior Union commander on the field went from one of the Union's best (John Reynolds) to one of the Union's weakest (Oliver Otis Howard).

SCENARIO SPECIFIC RULES

SCENARIO LENGTH

The scenario starts with the beginning of the 2 p.m. turn and continues until the end of the 4 p.m. turn for a total of four turns, or if the Confederates wish to see if they can win a grand tactical victory, the scenario can be extended to the end of the 5 p.m. turn for a total of six turns.

4 P.M. GAME, VICTORY CONDITIONS

For the Confederates to win a tactical victory in this scenario, by the end of the 4 p.m. turn no Union unit can be on the highest levels of McPherson's Ridge south of the unfinished railroad grade and north of the Fairfield Road – the Confederates must occupy it all. For the Union to win they must prevent that. Historically, the Confederates won, since by 4 p.m. all the Federal forces had retreated to Seminary Ridge to rebuild their defense.

5 P.M. GAME, VICTORY CONDITIONS

For the Confederates to win a grand tactical victory in this scenario, they must clear all the Federals off Seminary Ridge south of the unfinished railroad cut by the end of the 5 p.m. turn. For the Union to win they must prevent that. Had Seminary Ridge been cleared without the commitment of Pender's powerful division that would have left Pender's entire division as a fresh and undamaged formation that could have immediately moved against Cemetery Hill and perhaps even cut off the fleeing remnants of Howard's XI Corps. Had that happened, it is not unreasonable to assume that the ever-cautious General Meade would have assumed that the "delaying action" at Gettysburg was over, and that he should immediately prepare for the upcoming battle at Pipe Creek.

SCENARIO INITIATIVE

The historical scenario assumes that General Reynolds has been killed, and therefore the Confederates have the initiative. It remains unclear as to what killed General Reynolds: possibilities are a Confederate sharpshooter or simply that he was unlucky enough to catch one of the thousands of musket balls that were flying around. Nevertheless, he did have a dangerous habit of leading from the front, and given the close fighting in the woods along Willoughby Run it was probably an even chance that he would become a casualty. If desired, in order to decide at random if this scenario is played with him alive or dead, roll a **1D6** prior to the start of the scenario. If the result is 4, 5 or 6, assume that Reynolds has been previously shot and is no longer in command. If the result is 1, 2, or 3, assume that he survived and use the following variant of the scenario. If it has been determined that he starts the scenario alive, he would start "up front" on McPherson's Ridge; then use the normal officer casualty rules for the remainder of the scenario.

SCENARIO VARIANT - IF REYNOLDS IS STILL ALIVE

This version of the scenario uses the same setup, with the following modifications:

- Prior to the start of the first turn, the Union player has one free half action, worth a half movement, that can be used to move, reposition or change formation of any of his units. However this half action cannot be used to fire.
- If Reynolds has survived, the scenario initiative is decided at the beginning of each turn by a **1D6** competitive die roll, with the side with the highest number deciding which side

WHEN THE OBVIOUS IS NOT...

The disjointed nature of the Union positions on McPherson's Ridge had not gone unnoticed, and Major General Abner Doubleday – who had taken over I Corps following Reynolds' death – correctly felt that the wisest course would be to abandon the position before the Confederates swarmed on to them and to rebuild the Federal line on Seminary Ridge. Doubleday then sent Major Halstead to General Howard – the new left wing commander – to ask permission to immediately retire to Seminary Ridge. To emphasize the danger, Major Halstead pointed out to Howard a growing line of Confederate troops that were about to overlap the forward positions of the I Corps. Howard quickly barked back that "those are nothing but fence posts!" And then to prove his point, Howard ordered an aide to focus his binoculars on the "objects" and report exactly what he saw. After a few moments the ashen-faced aide lowered the glasses and said, "General, those are long lines of the enemy." Despite the now obvious evidence, Howard would not approve the retreat. Instead he instructed Halstead to tell Doubleday, "You may find Buford and use him."

can decide the initiative for this turn. If the competitive die roll is a tie, the Confederates have the initiative for this turn, or if during the scenario General Reynolds is killed, then the Confederates have the initiative for the remainder of the scenario.

CONFEDERATE INFANTRY

Davis' and Archer's brigades have taken heavy losses in the earlier fighting along Willoughby Run. Roll 2D6 for each brigade and that is the number of figures they have lost, to be spread out as evenly as possible among the constituent regiments. Due to their defeat this morning they have a +1 MMP modifier to their morale. Also, if doubles are rolled for their brigade, then that brigade has also lost its leader and suffers an additional +1 MMP morale modifier for any previous leader lost.

CONFEDERATE ARTILLERY

Visibility for Pegram and McIntosh's batteries on Herr Ridge is limited to any enemy unit on or anywhere west of McPherson's Ridge, anywhere on the western slopes of Oak Hill and on the highest level of Seminary Ridge. Union units between the highest levels of McPherson Ridge and Seminary Ridge are considered to be in "blind zones" and cannot be fired at. Likewise, Union units behind the high ground of Seminary Ridge cannot be fired at by the Confederate guns on Herr Ridge. Pegram and McIntosh's gun battalions have the historical restraint that they are fixed on Herr Ridge and may not move.

OPTIONAL ARTILLERY RELEASE

Roll a 1D6 for release by battery at the start of the first and second Confederate active turn (. and 2:30 p.m.). With a roll of 1, that battery is released and may freely redeploy. Historically, only Bander's battery was temporarily released for a slight forward deployment.

UNION INFANTRY

Meredith's and Cutler's brigades have taken moderate losses. Roll a 1D6 for each brigade to give the number of figures they have lost, to be spread out as evenly as practical among the various regiments.

UNION ARTILLERY

Both Hall's battery and Calef's horse artillery battery have had a rough morning dueling against the more numerous Confederate batteries. Prior to the start of the scenario, roll a 1D6 for both Hall's and Calef's battery. If it is a high roll (4, 5 or 6), that battery has lost a section.

UNION CAVALRY

Gamble's Brigade has taken slight losses. Roll a 1D6 for the brigade to give the number of figures they have lost, to be spread out evenly as practical among the various regiments. Also, due to hard fighting and fatigue, all units in Gamble's brigade have a +2 MMP morale modifier. Should any battalion of Gamble's brigade fail a morale check and go shaken or routed, that battalion and its entire parent regiment withdraws off the board and is removed from the game. Following the morning fight, Gamble had been pulled back as a dismounted reserve and consequently must stay dismounted to conserve the horses and cannot advance off Seminary Ridge. However, he can redeploy anywhere as dismounted cavalry along Seminary Ridge.

The death of General Reynolds, by Adam Hook © Osprey Publishing Ltd. Taken from Campaign 52: Gettysburg 1863.

Heth's attack is thrown back in confusion. (Patrick LeBeau & Chris Ward)

HISTORICAL OUTCOME

Historically, the Confederates swept the field, as the death of General Reynolds created serious leadership gaps in the Union defense. Meredith's "Iron Brigade" was left holding an exposed forward position on the east edge of Willoughby Run with unsecured flanks, with the other Union units unable to provide mutual support. The least experienced brigade of the Third Division that had been commanded by Brigadier General Thomas Rowley was now being led by the brave but somewhat untried Colonel Chapman Biddle, as the death of Reynolds resulted in Rowley assuming divisional command. Unfortunately, neither Biddle nor anyone else in the Third Division would receive useful guidance from General Rowley, as he spent most of the day being drunk and spouting irrelevant commands. Once Meredith's Iron Brigade was forced to retreat, the rest of the Union positions were defeated in detail, and despite some heroic last stands by individual units, soon all the Federals were quickly running eastward to form a stronger position on Seminary Ridge.

SUMMARY ORDER OF BATTLE

(For brigade, regiment and battery details see Army List)

THE UNION FORCES

Left Wing/I Corps – Major General Thomas Reynolds (2 LB)

If General Reynolds has been killed, substitute Major General Abner Doubleday (1 LB).

1st Cavalry Division, 1st Brigade
- Gamble's Cavalry Brigade
- Calef's Battery

I Corps/1st Division – Brigadier General James S. Wadsworth (1 LB)
- Meredith's – 1st Brigade, Brigadier General Solomon Meredith (1 LB) (9.30 a.m.)
- Cutler's – 2nd Brigade, Brigadier General Lysander Cutler (1 LB) (arrives 9 a.m.)

IMPACT OF REYNOLD'S DEATH

Since Reynolds was both the Left Wing commander and the I Corps commander, his death caused a dramatic ripple effect through the command structures of both I and XI Corps just as the battle was starting.

Command Position	Before Reynold's Death	After Reynold's Death
Senior Field Commander	Major General John Reynolds	Major General Oliver Otis Howard
Left Wing	Major General John Reynolds	Major General Oliver Otis Howard
I Corps	Major General John Reynolds	Major General Abner Doubleday
3rd Division/I Corps	Major General Abner Doubleday	Brigadier General Thomas Rowley
1st Brigade/3rd Division	Brigadier General Thomas Rowley	Colonel Chapman Biddle
121st Pennsylvania Regiment	Colonel Chapman Biddle	Major A. Biddle
XI Corps	Major General Oliver Otis Howard	Major General Carl Schurz
3rd Division/XI Corps	Major General Carl Schurz	Brigadier General A. Schimmelfenning
1st Brigade/3rd Division	Brigadier General A. Schimmelfenning	Colonel George von Amsberg
45th New York Regiment	Colonel George von Amsberg	Lt Col A. Dobke

I Corps/3rd Division – Major General Abner Doubleday (1 LB)

Brigadier General Thomas Rowley (No LB) if Reynolds was killed
- Biddle's – 1st Brigade – Colonel Chapman Biddle (1 LB)
- Stone's – 2nd Brigade – Colonel Roy Stone (1 LB)

I Corps Artillery Brigade – Colonel Charles Wainwright (1 Artillery LB)
- Stewart's Battery
- Hall's Battery
- Stevens' Battery
- Cooper's Battery
- Reynolds' Battery

THE CONFEDERATE FORCES

III Corps – Lieutenant General Ambrose Powell Hill (1 LB)
Heth's Division – Major General Henry Heth (No LB)
- Archer's Brigade – Brigadier General James Archer (1 LB)
- Davis Brigade – Brigadier General Joseph Davis (no LB)
- Pettigrew's Brigade – Brigadier General James Pettigrew (1 LB)
- Brockenbrough's Brigade – Colonel John Brockenbrough (1 LB)

III Corps Reserve Artillery
Pegram's Artillery Battalion – Major William Pegram (+1 Artillery LB)
- Johnson's Battery
- Marye's Battery
- Bander's Battery
- Zimmerman's Battery
- McGraw's Battery

McIntosh's Artillery Battalion – Major D. G. McIntosh (1 LB)
- Rice's Battery
- Hurt's Battery
- Wallace's Battery
- Johnson's Battery

II Corps

If playing the combined "McPherson's Ridge" with "Barlow's Knoll" scenario, Daniel's Brigade can enter at 2.30 p.m. on either board.
- Daniel's Brigade – Brigadier General Junius Daniel (1 LB)

SEMINARY RIDGE

3.30 p.m.–6 p.m., July 1, 1863 – Northwest of Gettysburg

THE CONFEDERATE SITUATION

"Here the brigade encountered a most terrific fire of grape and shell ... every discharge made sad havoc in our lines." – Brigadier General Alfred Scales, Brigade Commander, Pender's Division

Clearing McPherson's Ridge of the Federals had taken Heth longer than expected, and although Pender's Division had not been needed, the tough fighting had exhausted Heth's Division. The next ridge position – the one with the Seminary – that the Union had fallen back to looked significantly stronger yet. Looking though his binoculars at the Federal position, Major General A. P. Hill counted at least 20 well-positioned Federal guns and in some places it appeared that they might have thrown up some hasty works. This would not be work suitable for a tired division, so Pender was ordered to take the lead, with Heth's Division serving as a reserve and staying ready in the rear if needed. Looking to the north, Hill could see that Rodes was definitely making progress on the Federal flank, so perhaps one good, hard attack would send the enemy running. The orders were given. Pender's Division would move up and pass through Heth's Division; then Scales' North Carolinians would attack on the left, Perrin's South Carolinians would go up the middle, and Lane's Brigade would sweep up the right, where the Union flank looked vulnerable as it seemed to be anchored with only a cavalry brigade.

THE UNION SITUATION

"Tell General Doubleday that I don't know a damned thing about strategy, but we are giving the Rebels hell with these guns and I want to give them a few more shots before we leave!" – Colonel Charles Wainwright, I Corps Artillery Brigade Commander

Though Seminary Ridge position was potentially strong, with just enough elevation and slope that the Union artillery could fire over their infantry, none of the troops defending this line were fresh. They were all tired, and some of the best brigades, such as Meredith's and Cutler's, had already suffered considerable casualties. Major General Abner Doubleday, who following the death of General Reynolds was running the I Corps, knew that in moments his line would almost certainly be attacked by a fresh Confederate

division. Even should he hold against the storm that he knew was coming against his front, the battle to the north did not seem to be going well – it was only a matter of time before he would be forced off the ridge. However, before he was forced to yield this position he was determined that he would make the Rebels pay dearly for it.

General Doubleday had not expected to be thrust into command of the I Corps, and was still upset that General Howard had insisted that his units remain on McPherson's Ridge even after the position was clearly untenable. Though many of his units had already had a tough day, he had a good position. He knew he could count on the proven veterans of Meredith's and Cutler's brigades, and Stone's "new" Pennsylvania "Bucktails" had stood up well in the their first real fight. Biddle's Brigade seemed a little nervous, but at least it had Gamble's cavalry to support its flank.

Doubleday's artillery chief, Colonel Wainwright, seemed invigorated by the fact that finally he would have more artillery than the Rebels in the battle for this ridge. All day he had been fighting against massed Confederate guns on the high ground of Herr Ridge, but now it seemed that they had neglected to bring those guns forward. It was mistake that he would make their infantry pay dearly for. Going from battery to battery, Wainwright made sure that their limber chests were full and where possible extra canister rounds were brought forward from the reserve caissons. They were now as ready as they would ever be. He could see a long three-brigade line passing through a forward line and advancing in perfect alignment towards his position.

SCENARIO SPECIFIC RULES

SCENARIO LENGTH

The scenario starts with the beginning of the 3.30 p.m. turn and continues until the end of the 6 p.m. turn, for a total of five turns.

VICTORY CONDITIONS

For the Confederates to win, by the end of the 6 p.m. turn no Union units can be on any part of Seminary Ridge south of the unfinished railroad grade and north of the

SEMINARY RIDGE - 3:30 PM TO 6:00 PM

THOMAS' BDE. - Beginning 4:00 PM roll 1D6 for availability, it takes a "1".

POGUE'S ARTY. BN. - Beginning 4:00 PM roll 1D6 for availability, it takes a "1".

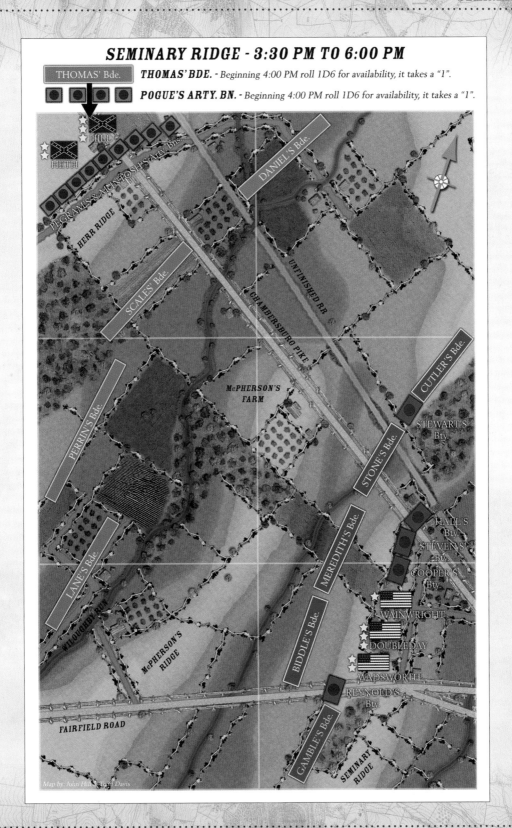

Map by: John Hill & Todd Davis

The Confederates turn the Union's Seminary Ridge line and begin to unravel it from south to north. (Patrick LeBeau & Chris Ward)

southern board edge – the Confederates must occupy it all. For the Union to win they must avoid that. Historically, the Confederates won, as by 6 p.m. all the Federal forces were fleeing through Gettysburg and beginning to rally on Cemetery Hill.

SCENARIO INITIATIVE
The historical scenario assumes that General Reynolds has been killed and that Major General Abner Doubleday is now in command of the I Corps. In that case, the Confederates have the initiative. If, however, General Reynolds is still alive, then the initiative is determined by a competitive 1D6 die roll with a tie going to the Confederates as Lee would now be on the field. To determine if Reynolds has survived, roll a 1D6 at the beginning of the scenario. If a 1 or 2 is rolled he is alive – anything else and he is dead.

CONFEDERATE INFANTRY

HETH'S DIVISION
They were on the field and were originally in front of Pender's Division. However, Heth's Division was exhausted and depleted from the McPherson's Ridge fight, and Pender's Division simply marched through the division and deployed in front of it. None of Heth's brigades would play a significant part in the Confederate

attack on Seminary Ridge. However, a few companies of both the 26th and 11th North Carolina regiments did attach themselves to other North Carolina regiments in Pender's Division. To indicate this, take one full stand from both the 26th and 11th North Carolina regiments and attach them to two other North Carolina units.

OPTIONAL - PENDER'S DIVISION - THOMAS' BRIGADE
Historically, Thomas' Brigade was held in reserve on Herr Ridge as infantry support for Pegram's and McIntosh's gun battalions throughout the day's battle. They saw no action. However, they could have been committed as follows. Beginning on the 4 p.m. turn and at the start of every following Confederate player turn, roll a 1D6 for the possible release of Thomas' Brigade. It takes a 1 for the brigade to be released, and if released they appear in line on Herr Ridge behind Pegram's and McIntosh's gun battalions and are now free to advance and engage at will.

CONFEDERATE ARTILLERY

PENDER'S DIVISION - POGUE'S ARTILLERY BATTALION
For the bulk of the fighting, Pogue's Artillery Battalion was kept in reserve and not brought forward until the battle was decided. To reflect this, roll 1D6 each turn, beginning with the Confederate portion of the 4 p.m.

turn, and if a 1 is rolled, Pogue's entire gun battalion arrives limbered on the Chambersburg Pike.

CONFEDERATE ARTILLERY VISIBILITY

Line of Sight visibility for Pegram and McIntosh's batteries is limited to any enemy unit on or anywhere west of McPherson's Ridge, anywhere on the western slopes of Oak Hill and on the highest level of Seminary Ridge. Union units between the highest levels of McPherson Ridge and Seminary Ridge are considered to be in "blind zones" and cannot be fired at. Likewise, Union units behind the high ground of Seminary Ridge cannot be fired at by the Confederate guns on Herr Ridge.

CONFEDERATE ARTILLERY RELEASE

The Confederate artillery cannot move off Herr Ridge until the Confederate turn after five non-depleted, non-shaken or non-routed Confederate regiments are standing on McPherson's Ridge from the Chambersburg Pike to the Fairfield Road. At that point, the Confederate artillery may roll a 1D6 for each battery once each turn for release. If released, the battery may freely redeploy to McPherson's Ridge. However, at no time in this scenario may the Confederate guns move beyond a supporting position on McPherson's Ridge. Historical Note: With the exception of Bander's Battery, which was temporarily moved forward, the Confederate guns were not moved off Herr Ridge until after Seminary Ridge was secured.

UNION RETREATS

If a routed Union unit's movement takes it to the edge of the table, it gets an immediate rally attempt. If it rallies, it stops where it is as a shaken unit. If it fails to rally, it is removed from the game.

UNION INFANTRY

Meredith's and Cutler's brigades have taken heavy losses. Prior to the start of the scenario, roll 2D6 for each brigade to give the number of figures they have lost, to be spread out as evenly as practical among the various regiments. They have also had a hard morning and their morale is worsened by a +2 MMP modifier. If doubles are rolled, then Meredith and/or Cutler were killed and are not included in this scenario, which raises the morale detriment to a +3 MMP modifier. Biddle's and Stone's infantry brigades have taken some losses; to give the number of figures those brigades have lost at the start of this scenario, roll a 1D6. In addition, due to having been driven off McPherson's Ridge, those brigades have a +1 MMP modifier to all their morale checks.

UNION ARTILLERY

Both Hall's Battery and Calef's Horse Artillery have had a rough morning dueling against the more numerous Confederate batteries. Prior to the start of the scenario, roll a 1D6 for both Hall's and Calef's battery. If a 3, 4 or 5 is rolled, that battery has lost a section. If however a 6 is rolled, then they have lost two sections, and are withdrawn off the board and unavailable for this scenario.

UNION CAVALRY

GAMBLE'S BRIGADE

Gamble's Brigade has taken slight losses. To give the number of figures it has lost, roll a 1D6 for the brigade; the losses are to be spread out evenly as practical among the various regiments. However, since the brigade was not directly involved in the final and futile defense of McPherson's Ridge, it has recovered somewhat from the stress of the morning, so that all units in Gamble's Brigade now only have a +1 MMP morale modifier. Nevertheless, should any battalion of Gamble's Brigade fail a morale check and go shaken or routed, that battalion and its entire parent regiment withdraws off the board and is removed from the game.

UNION CAVALRY RELEASE

As Lane's Brigade advanced, Gamble would remount the entire 8th Illinois and threaten the Confederate flank. To see if this occurs, roll a single 1D6 at the start of each Union active turn. If a 1 is rolled, then the Union player must immediately decide if he wishes to remount any one complete regiment and have it move freely as a mounted unit. However, since Gamble's orders were to stay on the flank, his units – mounted or dismounted – may not move north of the Fairfield Road. If on one of the following turns another 1, is rolled, then Gamble is only allowed to remount a single additional regiment in the scenario. Once one of Gamble's regiments has remounted, it must stay mounted for the rest of the scenario.

Historical Note: The order for Gamble to make a mounted demonstration came from Major General Winfield Hancock, who arrived on Cemetery Hill about 4.30 p.m. and immediately took charge of the chaos. The decision to remount the 8th Illinois and threaten the Confederate flank with a possible cavalry charge paid off handsomely. At least one regiment of Lane's Brigade panicked at the sight of the advancing horsemen and formed square, and the others immediately stopped advancing. Though Gamble's troop never charged – it was a bluff – the formed square made a great target for

"SEMINARY RIDGE"

There was no doubt that Major General Oliver O. Howard instinctively appreciated that Cemetery Hill south of Gettysburg was a vital position, and as the senior commander on the field, following Reynolds' death, he wanted the other generals to know that this was the position that must not fall. From Cemetery Hill, Howard could see the gray-clad infantry moving forward, and to emphasize his intent he grabbed an aide and ordered him to ride over to Seminary Ridge and inform the senior officer there that Cemetery Hill had to be held at all costs. The aide duly galloped off on his mission. Unfortunately, he was one of the many recent German immigrants that made up much of the XI Corps and only spoke a broken and most heavily accented English.

The senior officer that he found was Colonel Charles Wainwright, who commanded the I Corps artillery, and was organizing the guns for a delaying defense of Seminary Ridge. Wainwright, not having had the opportunity to go on to Cemetery Hill, was unaware that there was a cemetery there or anywhere else in the area. So when Howard's aide in broken German-English stressed that "Cemetery Hill" had to be held "at all hazards", Wainwright understood him to say "Seminary Hill", and so the defense of Seminary Ridge would become a "no retreat" last-stand type of defense rather than a more prudent delaying action.

Gamble's dismounted regiments that had the longer-ranged Sharps breechloading carbines. The net result was that Lane's Brigade contributed nothing to the assault on Seminary Ridge, which led the Confederate General Scales to comment that "Lane did not come up until the Yankees were clear out of reach."

UNION BREASTWORKS

There is evidence that a portion of the Federal position on Seminary Ridge was protected by hasty works. To reflect this, any one-brigade position is allowed to be protected by a line of hasty works on Seminary Ridge.

HISTORICAL OUTCOME

Though the Union infantry brigades on Seminary Ridge had been battered and driven off McPherson's Ridge, most of their artillery was relatively unscathed and was well positioned to pour shot, shell and canister into the attacking Rebels. Scales' Brigade on the Confederate left would be advancing into the concentrated fire of three undamaged Union batteries (Stewart's, Stevens' and Cooper's) and one section of Reynold's battery before it would even get into musket range of the mixed survivors of Cutler's, Stone's and Meredith's brigades. The result was carnage, and in less than an hour Scale's Brigade was wrecked. That morning about 1,400 men were available for the assault, but by the evening the brigade was only able to muster about 500 effectives. With Scales' Brigade rebuffed with heavy losses and Lane's Brigade intimidated by the flashing sabers of one or two regiments of Gamble's cavalry brigade, that left only Perrin's four South Carolina regiments – with no artillery support – to carry the Ridge.

Fortunately for the Confederate attack, Perrin's South Carolinians faced Biddle's rather wobbly brigade and only two sections of Reynolds' Battery, which did not have adequate infantry support. The bulk of Biddle's Brigade held well enough, but it was just too far away to provide support for the four guns of Reynolds' Battery and the 1st South Carolina broke the seam between it and the 121st Pennsylvania. At that point, the entire Union line began to unravel from south to north. Despite instances of heroic resistance by individual companies, the Federal I Corps was beaten, and quickly its panicked survivors were joining their XI Corps comrades in a headlong retreat through the streets of Gettysburg, heading for Cemetery Hill and the safety of an even stronger position.

General Pender readies his division outside Herr Tavern to move forward and assault Seminary Ridge. (Malcolm Johnston)

A DEVASTATED BRIGADE

The prolonged fighting reduced the regiments of the Iron Brigade to shadows of their former strength, as follows:

Regiment	Engaged Strength	Total Losses	Percentage Loss
19th Indiana	308 men	210 men	68%
24th Michigan	496 men	363 men	73%
2nd Wisconsin	302 men	233 men	77%
6th Wisconsin	344 men	168 men	49%
7th Wisconsin	364 men	178 men	49%

SUMMARY ORDER OF BATTLE
(For brigade, regiment and battery details see Army List)

THE UNION FORCES

Left Wing/I Corps, Major General Reynolds (2 LB)
If General Reynolds has been killed, substitute Major General Abner Doubleday (1 LB)
1st Cavalry Division, 1st Brigade
• Gamble's Cavalry Brigade
• Calef's Battery

I Corps /1st Division – Brigadier General James S. Wadsworth (1 LB)
• Meredith's – 1st Brigade, Brigadier General Solomon Meredith (1 LB) (9.30 a.m.)
• Cutler's – 2nd Brigade, Brigadier General Lysander Cutler (1 LB) (arrives 9 a.m.)

I Corps/3rd Division – Major General Abner Doubleday (1 LB)
Brigadier General Thomas Rowley (No LB) if Reynolds was killed
• Biddle's – 1st Brigade – Colonel Chapman Biddle (1 LB)
• Stone's – 2nd Brigade – Colonel Roy Stone (1 LB)

I Corps Artillery Brigade – Colonel Charles Wainwright (1 Artillery LB)
• Stewart's Battery
• Hall's Battery
• Stevens' Battery
• Cooper's Battery
• Reynolds' Battery

THE CONFEDERATE FORCES

III Corps, Lieutenant General Ambrose Powell Hill (1 LB)
Pender's Division – Major General William Dorsey Pender (1 LB)
• Perrin's Brigade – Colonel Abner Perrin (1 LB)
• Lane's Brigade – Brigadier General James Lane (No LB)
• Scales' Brigade – Brigadier General Alfred Scales (1 LB)
• Thomas' Brigade – Brigadier General Edward Thomas (1 LB)
Roll for availability, from 4:00 p.m. on, each turn starting with the Confederate active portion of the 4 p.m. turn. Roll 1D6 – on a 1, Thomas' Brigade appears behind the gun battalions on Herr Ridge.

Pender's Divisional Artillery Battalion – Major William Pogue (1 LB)
Roll for availability from 4:00 p.m. on. On a 1D6 roll of 1, they appear limbered on Chambersburg Pike.
• Wyatt's Battery
• Graham's Battery
• Ward's Battery
• Brooke's Battery

II Corps
• Daniel's Brigade – Brigadier General Junius Daniel (1 LB)

ALONG THE CHAMBERSBURG PIKE

8 a.m.–2 p.m., July 1, 1863 – Northwest of Gettysburg

"Reynolds, who probably never received the Pipe Creek circular, was eager for the conflict and as his collision with Heth assumed the dimensions of a battle and it caused an immediate concentration of both armies at Gettysburg." – Brigadier General Henry Hunt, Chief of Artillery, Army of the Potomac

Napoleon once said that his generals and marshals could ask anything of him but time. Time was a precious commodity on July 1, 1863, and despite the Confederate mishandling of their concentration, they had achieved the time advantage and were building a decisive infantry and artillery superiority with every passing hour. Along the Chambersburg Pike, the hard knock that sent Archer's and Davis' Confederate brigades reeling back was quickly becoming ephemeral in its effect as the rest of Heth's Division and all of Pender's Division began shaking out from their line of march into battle order. By noon, Heth's two fresh brigades (Pettigrew and Brockenbrough) were ready to move forward, and Pender's four brigades were at hand to provide a continual escalating assault along with ample artillery support from the high ground of Herr Ridge. A. P. Hill's two divisions were in an almost perfect position, as General Bedford Forrest would advise, "to keep up the scare." But at noon, the fighting became quiet, with only an artillery duel ongoing, and for two hours generals Heth and Hill waited for guidance from General Lee. The hard-pressed I Corps of the Army of the Potomac was given the welcome gift of time – about two hours of no assaults.

Lee had made it clear that he did not want to bring on a general engagement until he was sure of how much of the Army of the Potomac he was facing. At this moment, the Army of Northern Virginia's III Corps had the advantage of time as they were massing quicker than the Federals opposite them. It is always risky for corps and division commanders to seize the initiative and operate beyond the commander's intent, but this was exactly what generals Henry Heth, William Dorsey Pender and A. P. Hill needed to do. Not a reckless rush forward, but a consistent building of battlefield pressure

that could potentially transform a tactical victory into a strategic one that, with luck, could have enough political impact to weaken Federal resolve.

This scenario assumes that General A. P. Hill rode forward to Herr Ridge and saw that the resistance appeared to be Army of the Potomac cavalry – not Pennsylvania militia – and that the growing dust clouds south of Gettysburg probably indicated that its formidable infantry was not far behind. With that thought, he decided that it might be wiser to move forward in force rather than piecemeal. Since General Lee has emphasized caution, he would still hold Anderson's five-brigade division and its artillery battalion back as a reserve. Hill reasons that Heth's and Pender's divisions should be more than adequate to punch through whatever resistance they might encounter, militia or otherwise. With that decided, this scenario assumes that he would have given the orders for those two divisions to attack by brigade in an escalating assault as soon as their commanders have them in position.

For the Union, the I Corps brigades of Colonel Stone and Brigadier General Baxter – which were historically sent north to check Robert Rodes' division – are retained here along the Chambersburg Pike as the logical response to a Confederate pressure that would be more consistent and unrelenting than it actually was, since as yet Ewell had not arrived and there was no crisis to the north. This scenario is a classic matchup of a single Union Corps against two Confederate divisions.

SCENARIO SPECIFIC RULES

SCENARIO SETUP

This scenario starts with the exact same setup as does "The Devil to Pay" and continues from there.

SCENARIO LENGTH

This scenario starts with the 8 a.m. turn and ends with

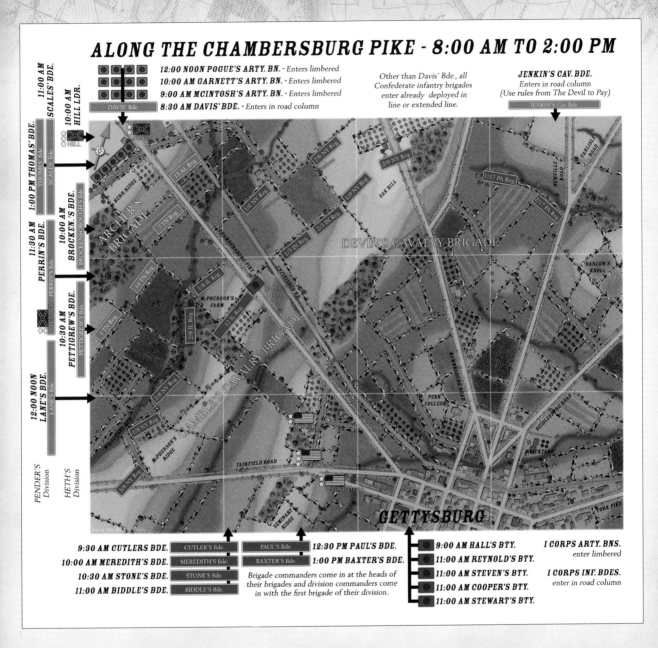

ALONG THE CHAMBERSBURG PIKE - 8:00 AM TO 2:00 PM

12:00 NOON POGUE'S ARTY. BN. - Enters limbered
10:00 AM GARNETT'S ARTY. BN. - Enters limbered
9:00 AM MCINTOSH'S ARTY. BN. - Enters limbered
8:30 AM DAVIS' BDE. - Enters in road column

Other than Davis' Bde., all Confederate infantry brigades enter already deployed in line or extended line.

JENKIN'S CAV. BDE.
Enters in road column
(Use rules from The Devil to Pay)

9:30 AM CUTLERS BDE.   CUTLER'S Bde.   PAUL'S Bde.   12:30 PM PAUL'S BDE.   9:00 AM HALL'S BTY.   I CORPS ARTY. BNS. enter limbered
10:00 AM MEREDITH'S BDE. MEREDITH'S Bde. BAXTER'S Bde.   1:00 PM BAXTER'S BDE.   11:00 AM REYNOLD'S BTY.
10:30 AM STONE'S BDE.   STONE'S Bde.   11:00 AM STEVEN'S BTY.   I CORPS INF. BDES. enter in road column
11:00 AM BIDDLE'S BDE.   BIDDLE'S Bde.   11:00 AM COOPER'S BTY.
                         Brigade commanders come in at the heads of   11:00 AM STEWART'S BTY.
                         their brigades and division commanders come
                         in with the first brigade of their division.

the conclusion of the 2 p.m. turn, for a total of 12 turns. Unlike the historical July 1 battle there is no battlefield lull from 12 noon until 2 p.m. Both sides can be as aggressive as they wish.

VICTORY CONDITIONS

For the Confederates to win, by the end of the 2 p.m. turn no Union units can be on any part of the highest level of Seminary Ridge south of the unfinished railroad grade and north of the southern board edge – the Confederates must occupy it all. For the Union to win, they must avoid that. Historically, the Confederates would take Seminary Ridge by 6 p.m. with heavy casualties, particularly in Scales' Brigade. However, had they cleared it by 2 p.m. – four hours earlier – then there may very well have been time, daylight and troops enough to clear Gettysburg and mount a "practicable" assault on Cemetery Hill.

Scale is an illusion. Though the figures are 15mm, the 6mm buildings look right for this terrain. (Patrick LeBeau & Chris Ward)

SCENARIO INITIATIVE

As long as General Reynolds is alive, the Union has the initiative until the start of the 1 p.m. turn, when General Lee has arrived, and from then on the initiative is decided by a competitive 1D6 die roll, with a tie going to the Confederates. If, however, at any time in the scenario should General Reynolds be killed, then the initiative shifts to the Confederates, beginning with the next turn and continuing through the rest of the scenario.

CONFEDERATE INFANTRY

Archer's Brigade of Heth's Division has been skirmishing with Buford's cavalry since early morning, and hence it does not have an opening volley benefit. Each brigade commander starts or enters the scenario attached to any one of his regiments. General Heth starts on Herr Ridge. General Pender can enter with any of his brigades. Corps commander General A. P. Hill enters on Herr Ridge on the 11 a.m. turn. Historically, Thomas' Brigade of Pender's Division was held back as a reserve, but in this scenario it is released, though it is the last unit of Pender's Division to be so.

CONFEDERATE ARTILLERY

CONFEDERATE ARTILLERY RELEASE

The Confederate artillery cannot move off Herr Ridge until the Confederate turn after all Union units have been driven off all parts of lower McPherson's Ridge from the Chambersburg Pike to the Fairfield Road. At that point, the Confederate artillery may freely redeploy to McPherson's Ridge. However, at no time in this scenario may they move beyond McPherson's Ridge. In the actual battle, the Confederate guns were not moved forward from Herr Ridge until after Seminary Ridge had been secured, and thereby deprived Pender's division of any artillery support when it attacked that ridge. Both Garnett's and Pogue's artillery battalions were also, for the most part, kept in reserve. In this scenario both are released for combat at what would have been an appropriate historical time.

CONFEDERATE ARTILLERY VISIBILITY

Line of Sight (LOS) for Pegram and McIntosh's batteries on Herr Ridge is limited to any enemy unit on or anywhere west of McPherson's Ridge, anywhere on the western slopes of Oak Hill and on the highest level of Seminary Ridge. Union units between the highest levels of McPherson Ridge and Seminary Ridge are considered to be in "blind zones" and cannot be fired at. Likewise, Union units behind the high ground of Seminary Ridge cannot be fired on by the Confederate guns on Herr Ridge.

UNION CAVALRY

All Union cavalry starts dismounted. The 17th Philadelphia starts behind the stream and cannot advance beyond it. By this time Buford's cavalry brigades and Calef's Horse Artillery Battery were exhausted and beginning to run low on ammunition. To reflect this, they have a +1 MMP additional modifier to all morale checks and an additional -1 DRM to all their fires until the start of the midnight turn, when these penalties increase to +2 MMP for morale and -2 DRM for firing. These modifiers are over and above the two worst modifier restriction. Also, since the cavalry has been skirmishing all morning, it does not get any opening volley benefits. Beginning with the start of the 10 a.m. turn, every Union cavalry battalion and Calef's Horse Artillery Battery must roll a 1D6 for immediate withdrawal as the Union infantry comes on to the battlefield. It takes a 5 or 6 for the cavalry units or Calef's battery to withdraw. For the Union cavalry withdrawal, if a 6 is rolled the unit is spent and it withdraws out of the scenario, but if a 5 is rolled the unit retires to Gettysburg as a reserve. Starting with its next active turn, it can be used anywhere on that board. However, since it is considered to be a voluntary withdrawal, there is no morale detriment "for element removed" against the rest of the brigade. It is assumed that the brigade commanders, colonels William Gamble and Thomas Devin, will stay on the board until their last unit withdraws and that the division commander, General John Buford, will remain until all the cavalry units have departed, at which time he will also leave.

When Calef's Battery withdraws, it retires to Seminary Ridge where it must remain until the start of the 10 p.m. turn, when Calef may return to the fight and deploy freely. At that time it is assumed that it has refilled its limber chests from the I Corps Artillery Brigade, which arrived at 11 a.m., and consequently when Calef's Battery returns to the fight it no longer has the -1 DRM firing detriment for low ammunition.

HISTORICAL OUTCOME

Since this is not a strict "historical" scenario, it does not have a strict "historical" result. However, that does not preclude reasonable historical speculation as to what might have followed using only the troops that were available and with only the time line changing. The most obvious result is that if Seminary Ridge had fallen two or three hours earlier, this may have given the Confederates enough time and fresh units to take either Culp's Hill or Cemetery Hill. That certainly is a good possibility, assuming that Union did nothing different. However, an accelerated Confederate attack may have spurred an accelerated Union response. Both III Corps and XII Corps were within an afternoon's march and both had been urged by generals Reynolds and Howard to come up At that point, the speculative equation changes and it becomes much more difficult to predict the sequence of events. If the Confederates do decisively prevail, then perhaps the most likely result would be that Meade activates the Pipe Creek option, which in turn throws the next decision back onto Robert E. Lee: whether to attack the Army of the Potomac in a strong position of its choice, or to ignore it and wait for the political pressure from Washington to force Meade to come up and attack him. Obviously, from then on, the timeline becomes unpredictable.

SUMMARY ORDER OF BATTLE
(For brigade, regiment and battery details see Army List)

THE UNION FORCES

Left Wing/I Corps, Major General Reynolds (2 LB)
   If General Reynolds has been killed, substitute Major General Abner Doubleday (1 LB).
1st Cavalry Division, 1st Brigade
- Gamble's Cavalry Brigade
- Calef's Battery

I Corps /1st Division – Brigadier General James S. Wadsworth (1 LB)
- Meredith's – 1st Brigade, Brigadier General Solomon Meredith (1 LB) (arrives 9.30 a.m.)
- Cutler's – 2nd Brigade, Brigadier General Lysander Cutler (1 LB) (arrives 9 a.m.)

I Corps/2nd Division – Brigadier General John Robinson (1 LB)
- Paul's – 1st Brigade – Brigadier General Gabriel Paul (No LB) (Arrives 12 noon)
- Baxter's – 2nd Brigade – Brigadier General Henry Baxter (1 LB) (Arrives 12.30 p.m.)

I Corps/3rd Division – Major General Abner Doubleday (1 LB)

Brigadier General Thomas Rowley (No LB) if Reynolds was killed

- Biddle's – 1st Brigade – Colonel Chapman Biddle (1 LB) (Arrives 11 a.m.)
- Stone's – 2nd Brigade – Colonel Roy Stone (1 LB) (Arrives 10.30 a.m.)

I Corps Artillery Brigade – Colonel Charles Wainwright (1 Artillery LB)

All batteries on field by 11 a.m.

- Stewart's Battery
- Hall's Battery
- Stevens' Battery
- Cooper's Battery
- Reynolds' Battery

THE CONFEDERATE FORCES

Pender's Division – Major General William Dorsey Pender (1 LB)

- Perrin's Brigade – Colonel Abner Perrin (1 LB)
- Lane's Brigade – Brigadier General James Lane (No LB)
- Scales' Brigade – Brigadier General Alfred Scales (1 LB)
- Thomas' Brigade – Brigadier General Edward Thomas (1 LB) – 3 p.m.

Pender's Divisional Artillery Battalion – Major William Pogue – 2 p.m.

- Wyatt's Battery
- Graham's Battery

- Ward's Battery
- Brooke's Battery

Heth's Division – Major General Henry Heth (No LB)

- Archer's Brigade – Brigadier General James Archer (1 LB)
- Davis' Brigade – Brigadier General Joseph Davis (no LB)
- Pettigrew's Brigade – Brigadier General James Pettigrew (1 LB)
- Brockenbrough's Brigade – Colonel John Brockenbrough (1 LB)

Heth's Divisional Artillery, Garnett's Battalion – Lieutenant Colonel John Garnett (no LB) – 1 p.m.

- Grandy's Battery
- Lewis' Battery
- Maurin's Battery
- Moore's Battery

III Corps Reserve Artillery

Pegram's Artillery Battalion – Major William Pegram (+1 Artillery LB)

- Johnson's Battery
- Marye's Battery
- Bander's Battery
- Zimmerman's Battery
- McGraw's Battery

McIntosh's Artillery Battalion – Major D. G. McIntosh (1 LB)

- Rice's Battery
- Hurt's Battery
- Wallace's Battery
- Johnson's Battery

Union XII Corps infantry arrive as Devin's cavalry brigade departs. (Patrick LeBeau & Chris Ward)

BARLOW'S KNOLL

2–5 p.m., July 1, 1863 – North of Gettysburg

"He had misunderstood my orders, or that he was carried away by the ardor of the conflict." – Major General Carl Schurz, temporary commander, XI Corps

Brigadier General Francis Barlow was a recent addition to XI Corps, having just joined in May of 1863. He had been brought over to the XI Corps by its commander, Major General Oliver Otis Howard, to rebuild the fighting spirit of its First Division following its rout at Chancellorsville. Barlow was an experienced, tough and stubborn fighter who welcomed the upcoming fight as an opportunity to redeem the reputation of both his division and the XI Corps. Upon arriving at the battlefield, his brigades were immediately taken under fire by the Confederate guns on Oak Hill as they debauched from Gettysburg. Though few men were killed, the fire was persistent and galling. Looking northward, Barlow saw a generally flat plain with only a few good artillery positions – the one exception being a gently rising knoll that was part of the Blocher Farm along Rock Creek. Barlow's consternation concerning this knoll increased as he spotted Confederate skirmishers taking position on it. Barlow instinctively knew that this piece of high ground could prove critical in his plans to engage the flank of Robert Rodes' Confederate division to the north, and he was also seriously concerned that the Confederates might get a battery or two on it to threaten his right flank. Barlow claimed that he then sought permission to advance forward and seize this knoll before the Confederates reinforced their grip on it.

At this point, the responsibility for approving or ordering the advance to Blocher's Knoll – which would henceforth be forever known as Barlow's Knoll – becomes murky, as this movement would become the key mistake that would totally unhinge the XI Corps position. Believing that full permission to advance had been obtained, Barlow ordered Von Gilsa's Brigade and Wilkeson's Battery to occupy the knoll and drive off Doles' feisty battalion of sharpshooters, and then ordered Ames' Brigade to move up in support. Had Barlow only been facing Rodes' division – which was potent enough – occupying this knoll might have been an excellent move, as it would have anchored Barlow's right flank. To explore that possibility, play this scenario as presented, without introducing the impact of Early's division.

HISTORICAL OUTCOME

Unfortunately, Barlow's advance to Blocher's Knoll would instead have the disastrous effect of exposing the entire right flank of the XI Corps to Jubal Early's arriving division, which by 3 p.m. was moving forward to roll up the entire Union right flank. Historically that is exactly what happened. To recreate that historical situation, simply play this scenario and the "Slocum Arrives" scenarios together. Without the Union XII Corp units, it will be a most difficult day for Billy Yank. While Barlow probably did not know of the impending arrival of Early's division, General Howard, who with the death of General Reynolds was now the senior Union commander on the field, most certainly did. Earlier, Colonel Devin's cavalry brigade had been scouting northeast of Gettysburg and had reported to Howard that Early's Confederates were advancing in strength. It is unclear, however, if General Schurz, now commanding the XI Corps, had been informed and if an appropriate warning had been given to General Barlow. Unfortunately, General Barlow had been seriously wounded and taken prisoner in the subsequent debacle and never filed an official report. However, in a later letter to his wife he clearly stated that he was only following orders.

What if Early had not arrived to an uncontested field and caved in the flank of the XI Corps? Could Howard's XI Corps' "Dutchmen" have held off Rodes' superb division? That question is the subject of this scenario. This scenario can be played as a stand-alone fight, or it could be played in conjunction with the 2 p.m. XII Corps scenario, "Slocum Arrives," as the arrival of Brigadier General Alpheus Williams' Division of the XII Corps would certainly have slowed Early's flank attack against the XI Corps. Likewise, "Barlow's Knoll" could be played in conjunction with either the "McPherson's Ridge" scenario or the "Seminary Ridge" scenario from the "Chambersburg Pike" scenario series.

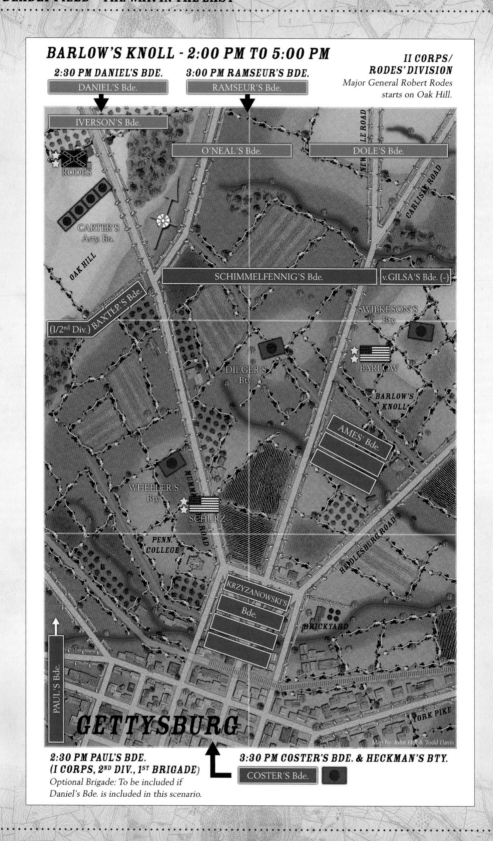

BARLOW'S KNOLL - 2:00 PM TO 5:00 PM

2:30 PM DANIEL'S BDE.

3:00 PM RAMSEUR'S BDE.

*II CORPS/
RODES' DIVISION*
Major General Robert Rodes
starts on Oak Hill.

DANIEL'S Bde.

RAMSEUR'S Bde.

IVERSON'S Bde.

O'NEAL'S Bde.

DOLE'S Bde.

RODES

CARTER'S
Arty. Bn.

OAK HILL

SCHIMMELFENNIG'S Bde.

v.GILSA'S Bde. (-)

(I/2ⁿᵈ Div.) BAXTER'S Bde.

WILKESON'S
Bty.

BARLOW

DILGER'S
Bty.

BARLOW'S
KNOLL

AMES' Bde.

WHEELER'S
Bty.

SCHURZ

PENN.
COLLEGE

KRZYZANOWSKI'S
Bde.

BRICKYARD

PAUL'S Bde.

GETTYSBURG

YORK PIKE

Map by John Hill & Todd Davis

2:30 PM PAUL'S BDE.
(I CORPS, 2ⁿᵈ DIV., 1ˢᵀ BRIGADE)
*Optional Brigade: To be included if
Daniel's Bde. is included in this scenario.*

3:30 PM COSTER'S BDE. & HECKMAN'S BTY.

COSTER'S Bde.

BARLOW'S KNOLL - 3:00 PM TO 5:00 PM

CARTER'S ARTY. BN. - Assume that with the 3:00 PM start Iverson's Brigade would prevent Carter's guns from firing on Baxter's Brigade, but Carter would be able to fire at any of the Union batteries.

In the 3:00 PM version of Barlow's Knoll, it is assumed that both Daniel's Confederate Brigade and Paul's Union Brigade were committed to the battle along the Chambersburg Pike on the West game board.

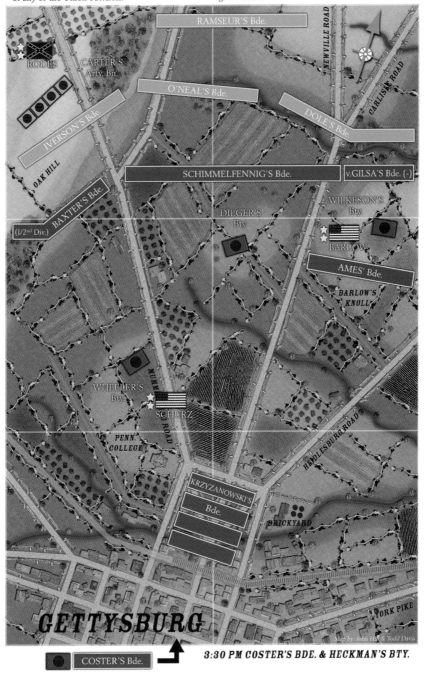

COMBINED SCENARIOS: "BARLOW'S KNOLL" AND "SLOCUM ARRIVES"

Normally, the 54th New York and the 153rd Pennsylvania regiments of Leopold von Gilsa's Brigade are used in the 2 p.m. version of "Slocum Arrives" scenario and are not available for "Barlow's Knoll." However, if the two scenarios are played in conjunction with each other, then those two regiments can be deployed on either game board. To win the combined scenario, the Confederates must meet the victory conditions of both scenarios. For the Union to win, they also have to win both scenarios. If each side wins one, then it is a draw. For this combined scenario, the game is extended to the end of the 6 p.m. turn.

EWELL ATTACKS - 2:00 PM TO 6:00 PM
COMBINES "BARLOW'S KNOLL 2 PM START" WITH "SLOCUM ARRIVES - 2 PM START"

2:30 PM DANIEL'S BDE.

3:00 PM RAMSEUR'S BDE.

II CORPS/ RODES' DIVISION
Major General Robert Rodes starts on Oak Hill.

All Confederate infantry brigades arrive deployed in line or extended line.

4:00 PM SMITH'S BDE.
3:00 PM HOKE'S BDE.
2:30 PM HAY'S BDE.
2:00 PM JONES ARTY. BN.
Arrives limbered.

2:00 PM GORDON'S BDE.

2:30 PM PAUL'S BDE.
(I CORPS, 2ND DIV., 1ST BRIGADE)
Optional Brigade: To be included if Daniel's Bde. is included in this scenario.

3:30 PM COSTER'S BDE. & HECKMAN'S BTY.

2:00 PM McDOUGALL'S BDE.
2:30 PM XII CORPS ARTY. BDE.
3:00 PM RUGER'S BDE.
4:00 PM LOCKWOOD'S BDE.

1ST DIV./XII CORPS
Brig. Gen. Alpheus Williams arrives with the XII Corps Arty. Bde.

All Union infantry brigades arrive in road column and artillery batteries arrive limbered.

COMBINED SCENARIOS: "BARLOW'S KNOLL" AND "MCPHERSON'S RIDGE"

If playing these as a combined scenario in conjunction with "McPherson's Ridge," the Confederate player has the option of bringing in Daniel's Brigade at 2.30 p.m. on either this board or on the top adjacent edge of the western game board. Likewise, the Union player has the option of bringing in Paul's Brigade on either this board or on the bottom adjacent edge of the western game board. To win the combined scenario, the Confederates must meet the victory conditions of both scenarios. For the Union to win, they also have to win both scenarios. If each side wins one, then it is a draw. For this combined scenario, the game is extended to the end of the 6 p.m. turn.

Regiments from Doles' Brigade gradually push the Federals off Barlow's Knoll. (Doug Kline)

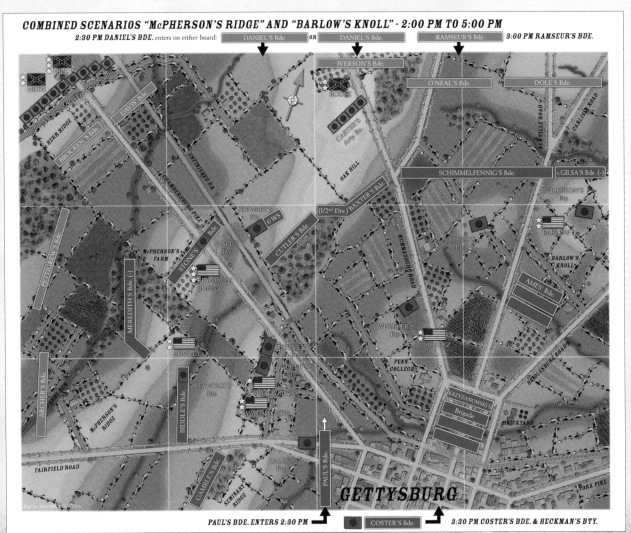

SCENARIO SPECIFIC RULES

INITIATIVE AND SCENARIO RESTRICTIONS

For "Barlow's Knoll" the Confederates have the initiative. If playing this scenario by itself, neither side may cross Rock Creek. If playing this scenario in conjunction with the "Slocum Arrives" scenario, then either side may cross Rock Creek with any of their units.

SCENARIO LENGTH

The scenario can be played with either a 2 p.m. or 3 p.m. start time and ends at 5 p.m. for a total of six or four turns. Historically, this battle was over by 5 p.m., but by mutual agreement the scenario could be extended to 6 p.m. If played as a combined scenario with either the "McPherson's Ridge" or the "Slocum Arrives" scenarios, the 6 p.m. turn is the last turn.

VICTORY CONDITIONS

For the Confederates to win the "Barlow's Knoll" scenario, they must have four regiments south of the York-Fairfield Road at the end of the last turn. The Union wins if they can prevent that. If playing this scenario in conjunction with one of the eastern board XII Corps scenarios, then the Confederate must get seven regiments anywhere south of the York-Fairfield Road by the end of the last turn to win. The Union wins if they can prevent that.

MARCH COLUMN RESTRICTIONS

If an infantry road column comes under any fire that results in a morale check, regardless of whether it passes the morale check or not, that road column must immediately use its next action or reaction to change into a battle formation. If it was moving as part of its second action and consequently would not have an action left, it simply stops and must use its next reaction to change into a battle formation.

ARTILLERY FIRE OVER INFANTRY

Union artillery can do non-canister fire over the heads of friendly units if the battery or the targeted unit is at least one elevation higher than the intervening friendly unit, provided that both the firing battery and the targeted unit are at least two inches from the intervening friendly unit. Confederate batteries can also fire over friendly units in the same manner, but either the battery or the target must be at least two elevations higher than the intervening friendly unit, and both the firing battery and the targeted unit have to be at least three inches from the intervening friendly unit.

SPECIAL TERRAIN

Just outside of Gettysburg was the brickyard, which was a complex of brick kilns and storage areas. It can hold up to two regiments or one battery, and any unit in the brickyard gets an additional +1 target DRM over and above the usual "best two" against infantry fire – but not artillery fire – and is entitled to the -1 MMP benefit for being in cover.

OPTIONAL - CONFEDERATE REDEPLOYMENT OPTION

Daniel's Brigade is optional, and if used enters at 2.30 p.m. either where Iverson's Brigade entered or behind where O'Neal's Brigade started. Ramseur's Brigade can enter at 3 p.m. as shown or anywhere on the northern board edge. If Daniel's Brigade is used, it is recommended that the Federals get Paul's Brigade.

CHARLES COSTER'S BRIGADE

The brigades of Colonel Charles Coster and Colonel Orlando Smith made up the second division of the XI Corps under Brigadier General Adolph Von Steinwehr. For the most part they were held back as a reserve on Cemetery Hill. Coster's Brigade and Heckman's Battery would eventually be released at about 3.30 p.m. in a futile last-ditch effort to halt Harry Hay's "Louisiana Tigers" and Avery's North Carolina brigades at the "brickyard" just northeast of Gettysburg.

ORLANDO SMITH'S BRIGADE

Historically, Colonel Orlando Smith's Brigade and Weidrich's Battery were kept back on Cemetery Hill throughout the first day and would become the foundation for the Union defense of that position that evening. As these were the last reserves of XI Corps and since General Howard was convinced that Cemetery Hill was the key position that must be held at all costs, this scenario assumes that it would have been most unlikely that they would have been released, so they are not included.

SUMMARY ORDER OF BATTLE
(For brigade, regiment and battery details see Army List)

THE UNION FORCES

XI Corps, Major General Oliver Otis Howard (1 LB)
Major General Oliver Otis Howard starts anywhere in Gettysburg

XI Corps/1st Division, Brigadier General Francis Barlow (1 LB)
- Von Gilsa's – 1st Brigade – Colonel Leopold Von Gilsa (1 LB)
  The 153rd PA & 54th NY are not available except in combined scenarios
- Ames' – 2nd Brigade – Brigadier General Adelbert Ames (1 LB)

XI Corps/2nd Division, Brigadier General Adolph Von Steinwehr (1 LB)
- Coster's – 1st Brigade – Colonel Charles Coster (1 LB)
- Smith's – 2nd Brigade – Colonel Orlando Smith (1 LB)
  Not available, remained on Cemetery Hill

XI Corps/3rd Division, Major General Carl Schurz (1 LB)
- Schimmelfennig's – 1st Brigade – Brigadier General A. Schimmelfennig (1 LB)
- Kryzanowski's – 2nd Brigade – Colonel Waldimir Krzyzanowski (1 LB)

XI Corps Artillery Brigade – Major Thomas Osborne (No arty LB)
- Wheeler's Battery
- Dilger's Battery
- Wilkeson's Battery
- Heckman's Battery (3.30 p.m.)
- Weidrich's Battery (Optional, 5 p.m.)

I Corps/2nd Division, Brigadier General John Robinson (1 LB)
General Robinson (1 LB) is available if both Paul's and Baxter's brigades are used in this scenario
- Paul's – 1st Brigade – Brigadier General Gabriel Paul (1 LB) – 2.30 p.m.
  Optional – to be used if Confederates elect to use Daniel's Brigade
- Baxter's – 2nd Brigade – Brigadier General Henry Baxter (1 LB)

THE CONFEDERATE FORCES

II Corps – Lieutenant General Richard S. Ewell (1 LB)
Lieutenant General Richard Ewell starts together with Major General Robert Rodes

II Corps/Rodes' Division, Major General Robert Rodes (1 LB)
- Doles' Brigade – Brigadier General George Doles (2 LB)
  For this scenario assume that Blackford's Sharpshooters are part of Doles' Brigade
- Daniel's Brigade – Brigadier General Junius Daniel (1 LB) – Optional
- Iverson's Brigade – Brigadier General Alfred Iverson (no LB)
- O'Neal's Brigade – Colonel Edward O'Neal (1 LB)
- Ramseur's Brigade – Brigadier General Stephen Ramseur (1 LB)

Rodes' Divisional Artillery Battalion – Lieutenant Colonel Thomas H. Carter
- Reese's Battery
- Carter's Battery
- Page's Battery
- Fry's Battery

SLOCUM ARRIVES

2/3 p.m.–6 p.m., July 1, 1863 – Northeast of Gettysburg

"The Corps could easily have joined in the battle the first day. The distance from our starting point to the battlefield might have been traversed by noon." – E. R. Brown, 27th Indiana Regiment, XII Corps

Two Taverns was a pleasant stop along the Baltimore Pike on the road to Gettysburg. Major General Henry W. Slocum had decided that it was an appropriate place to rest the Army of the Potomac's XII Corps, and for the past two hours that was what he and his corps had been doing. It was somewhat past noon – lunch time – and

since Two Taverns was only four to five miles from Gettysburg, should the new commander of the Army of the Potomac, Major General George C. Meade, order him and his corps forward to support what sounded like a growing battle, his corps would be rested and ready. However, as yet he had not received any clear-cut orders to advance, and Henry Slocum was a stickler for orders. Earlier that morning he had received an ambiguous discretionary order, which said "assume position for offensive or defensive, as occasion requires, or rest the

Early's Division advances on the just arriving XII Corps. (P. J. O'Neill)

SLOCUM ARRIVES
2:00 PM START

All Confederate infantry brigades arrive deployed in line or extended line.

4:00 PM SMITH'S BDE. SMITH'S Bde.

3:00 PM HOKE'S BDE. HOKE'S Bde.

2:30 PM HAY'S BDE. HAY'S Bde.

2:00 PM JONES ARTY. BN. *Arrives limbered.*

2:00 PM GORDON'S BDE. EARLY GORDON'S Bde.

17 VA Reg.

153 PA

5 NY Reg. 9 NY Reg.

XII Corps units 54 NY

BIGLERSBURG ROAD

RIDGE CREST LINE 27 PA Reg.

DEVIN'S CAVALRY BRIGADE

HUNTERSTOWN ROAD

RAILROAD

ROCK CREEK

HOSPITAL WOODS

YORK PIKE

WOLF'S HILL

1ST DIV./XII CORPS
Brig. Gen. Alpheus Williams arrives with the XII Corps Arty. Bde.

2:00 PM McDOUGALL'S BDE. McDOUGALL'S Bde.

2:30 PM XII CORPS ARTY. BDE.

WILLIAMS

3:00 PM RUGER'S BDE. RUGER'S Bde.

4:00 PM LOCKWOOD'S BDE. LOCKWOOD'S Bde.

All Union infantry brigades arrive in road column and artillery batteries arrive limbered.

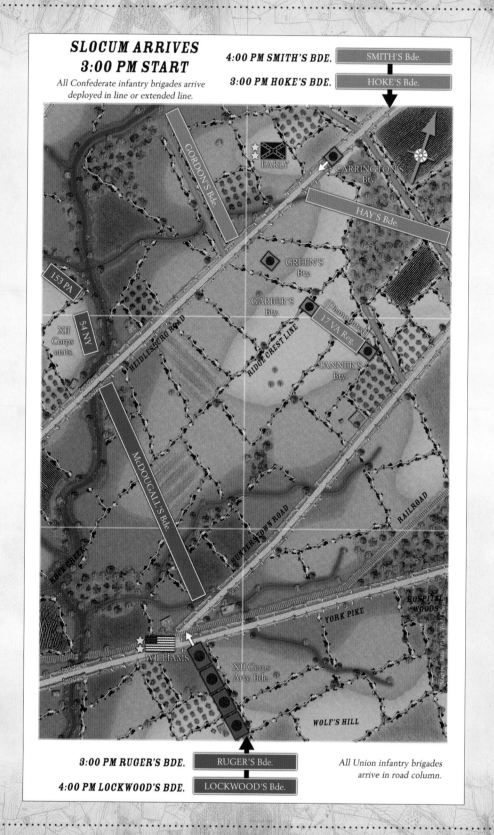

SLOCUM ARRIVES
3:00 PM START

All Confederate infantry brigades arrive deployed in line or extended line.

4:00 PM SMITH'S BDE.   SMITH'S Bde.

3:00 PM HOKE'S BDE.   HOKE'S Bde.

EARLY

CARRINGTON'S Bty.

GORDON'S Bde.

HAY'S Bde.

GREEN'S Bty.

153 PA

GARBER'S Bty.

17 VA Rgt. (Dismounted)

54 NY

XII Corps units.

HEIDLESBURG ROAD

RIDGE CREST LINE

TANNER'S Bty.

McDOUGALL'S Bde.

HUNTERSTOWN ROAD

RAILROAD

ROCK CREEK

HOSPITAL WOODS

YORK PIKE

WILLIAMS

XII Corps Arty Bde.

WOLF'S HILL

3:00 PM RUGER'S BDE.   RUGER'S Bde.

4:00 PM LOCKWOOD'S BDE.   LOCKWOOD'S Bde.

All Union infantry brigades arrive in road column.

troops." Prior to that he had received General Meade's Pipe Creek Circular, which to him strongly suggested that Meade's preferred plan was to fight a defensive battle along Pipe's Creek, and for that battle Henry Slocum would be acting as a wing commander with command over both the XII and the V Corps. With these two communiqués in hand, Henry Slocum chose the option to rest and wait for more direct orders from General Meade or from Meade's designated field commander, Major General John F. Reynolds, who, unknown to Slocum, was already two hours dead.

As the day wore on, the noise of battle increased and Slocum received two messages from Major General O. O. Howard, the commander of the Union XI Corps, that things were not going well and that he needed help. However, it was a request and not an order, and Slocum did not take orders from General Howard but from General Meade. So XII Corps continued to rest. By late afternoon, Slocum had received a message that whenever he finally arrived at the new Union position on Cemetery Hill, he would be in command of the field until General Meade arrived. With the news that he would in charge, he finally got the XII Corps on the road and even diverted its First Division under Brigadier General Alpheus S. Williams northward to support XI Corps' right flank. But it was too little and too late. By 6 p.m., Williams was in position to move on Wolf's or even Benner's Hill, but the battle was very much over and Howard's unlucky XI Corps had again been rolled up two hours earlier by Jubal Early's veteran Confederate division. With that sad news, Williams and his division was ordered to re-join the rest of the XII Corps on the Baltimore Pike.

BUT WHAT IF... SLOCUM WASN'T SLOW?

However, had Henry Slocum simply decided to march to the sound of the guns three hours earlier, he could easily have had Williams' First Division arriving on XI Corps flank by 3 p.m. Had that happened, Early's division would have had to turn and face Williams rather than easily steamrolling over Barlow's Knoll and the poorly deployed XI Corps. Would it have made a difference on the first day of Gettysburg? Maybe, as it probably would have bought enough time for XII Corps' second division also to get into the fight, and perhaps even the lead elements of other Corps. At best, it might have resulted in the first day ending in a draw rather than a tactical Confederate victory. This scenario assumes that Slocum orders

Williams' Division with the XII Corps Artillery Brigade forward to the right flank of XI Corps, in much the same way that was actually done, but three hours earlier. In reality, Lockwood's large green brigade did not arrive until the morning of July 2, but since this scenario assumes that XII Corps responded with more urgency, we have Lockwood arriving in the late afternoon on July 1.

TWO VERSIONS OF THE SCENARIO

Both the long and the short version of this scenario assume that rather than resting at Two Taverns, Henry Slocum orders XII Corps to march to the sound of the guns, and both use the exact same game board. However, they portray a very different situation and present the players with a different set of tactical challenges and opportunities.

SLOCUM ARRIVES - 2 P.M. TO 6 P.M.

This eight-turn version of the scenario starts with Devin's Cavalry Brigade, which after having fought all morning was now being called upon to fight again and to screen and delay Jubal Early's fresh division. Historically, Devin did not hold for long, but before he pulled out he did provide an unheeded warning that heavy forces were moving on the Federal XI Corps' flank. However, in this version of "Slocum Arrives," Devin has to hold for at least two turns to give the first division of the XII Corps under Brigadier General Alpheus Williams time to get into position to secure the flank of a very nervous XI Corps. This is an interesting situation, as it will require the Union player simultaneously to execute a delaying cavalry action against a fresh and aggressive infantry division while moving his own infantry division into place to check Early's advance. This version of the scenario can be played in conjunction with "Barlow's Knoll" or as part of the three-gameboard "A Long Afternoon" combined scenario, as both of those also start at 2 p.m. In this version of the scenario, the 17th Virginia Cavalry comes on the board mounted, leading Jones' Artillery Battalion.

SLOCUM ARRIVES - 3 P.M. TO 6 P.M.

This six-turn version of the scenario assumes that Devin's Cavalry Brigade did its job and delayed Early's Division just long enough that the lead elements of Williams' Division were able to get into position to hold the line until the other XII Corps artillery and the other brigades can get deployed. The shorter version of the scenario that does not require any Union cavalry figures and is completely contained on the one game board. In this

Devin sets up a cavalry screen as the Confederates cautiously probe forward. (Patrick LeBeau & Chris Ward)

version of the scenario, the 17th Virginia Cavalry starts dismounted, supporting Tanner's and Garber's batteries.

SCENARIO SPECIFIC RULES

SCENARIO INITIATIVE
Jubal Early's Confederate division has the initiative throughout the scenario.

SCENARIO SETUP
Within the indicated brigade areas, the respective player can set up the regiments in either battle line or extended line. Each full brigade that begins on the board may deploy one or two regiments as much as two inches forward as skirmishers and one regiment up to two inches back as a reserve. This option is not available for the two regiments from Von Gilsa's XI Corps brigade – the 54th New York and the 153rd Philadelphia. Arriving units are indicated. All Union infantry units enter in road column.

All Confederate infantry units enter in battle line or extended line. All batteries enter limbered.

RECOMMENDED OPTIONAL RULES
While gamers are free to use any, all, or none of the optional rules, the following rules are recommended for this scenario: variable entry time (2 p.m. scenario only), road column under fire, and artillery fire over infantry.

VICTORY CONDITIONS
If at the end of the last turn of the game, the Confederates have four regiments south of the York Pike and west of the Hospital Woods or across Rock Creek south of the Heidelsburg Road, they have won. The Union wins if the Confederates have two or fewer regiments south of the York Pike and west of the Hospital Woods or across Rock Creek. Anything in between is a draw. The Confederates may count any one regiment that is across Rock Creek north of the Heidelsburg Road towards their required five-regiment Victory Conditions.

SCENARIO RESTRICTIONS

The Confederates cannot cross Rock Creek north of the Heidelsburg Road until the 45th New York and the 153rd Philadelphia regiments have been driven off, and then only two regiments may cross north of the Heidelsburg Road – though, as noted, only one regiment will count towards the Confederate Victory Conditions.

26TH GEORGIA REGIMENT AS ARTILLERY SUPPORT

Historically, the 26th Georgia Regiment was detailed to support Jones' Artillery Battalion. To reflect this, the 26th Georgia must stay adjacent to the closest Confederate artillery battery until released. Roll 1D6 at the beginning of each Confederate active turn for release; it takes a 1 or 2 to be released. In the actual battle, the 26th Georgia was not released until the battle was almost over and the Union in full retreat. See similar rule for the 17th Virginia Cavalry.

COMBINED SCENARIO

If this scenario is combined with the "Barlow's Knoll" scenario, then the restriction against Early's units crossing Rock Creek does not apply. Likewise, in the combined scenario any XI Corps units from the Barlow's Knoll scenario are also free to cross Rock Creek on to this board.

2 P.M. SCENARIO - DEVIN'S CAVALRY BRIGADE

Due to previous fighting that morning, roll 1D6 for total figure losses for Devin's Cavalry Brigade. Distribute losses as equally as possible among the battalions and regiments. All units start dismounted in a cavalry line or skirmish order. Due to having being heavily engaged all morning, all Devin's battalions or regiments have a +2 MMP modifier due to fatigue and have no opening volley benefits. If any unit fails any morale check, it must remount and retire off the board via the York Pike. If any unit remounts, it must retire off the game board as detailed above. Once one complete regiment (both of the two battalions of the regiment) has begun to retire off the board for any reason, then all the rest of Devin's Brigade will immediately remount and also begin to retire off the board via the York Pike. Once a unit has retired, it is removed from the game. These rules also apply to the scenario when combined with the "Barlow's Knoll" or the "A Long Afternoon" scenario.

THE 17TH VIRGINIA CAVALRY

This cavalry regiment was detached from Jenkins' Brigade and was more mounted infantry or partisan rangers than trained cavalry. As cavalry, Jubal Early noted that "they were not well trained." They have eight figures with rifle muskets and fight as Veterans dismounted or as Green troops when mounted. They fire on the cavalry table with rifle muskets. If they attempt a mounted charge, it is all done in as Green troops in disorder. In the 2 p.m. scenario, once they dismount they must stay dismounted. In the 3 p.m. scenario, they are dismounted for the whole scenario. Historically on July 1, the 17th Virginia Cavalry was used mostly as support for Early's artillery. To reflect this, they must stay adjacent to one of the Confederate artillery batteries until released. At the beginning of each Confederate active turn, roll a 1D6 and they are released with the roll of a 1 or 2.

WILKESON'S BATTERY - ON BARLOW'S KNOLL

Off-board to the west on Barlow's Knoll, Wilkeson's Battery was trying to provide fire support both to Von Gilsa's two regiments on this board facing Gordon's Brigade, and the rest of Von Gilsa's Brigade that was facing Rodes' Division on the adjacent gameboard. To reflect this, any time the 54th New York or the 153rd Philadelphia fire, and the natural die roll before any modifiers is even, then that fire gets an extra +1 DRM for artillery support. However, if it was an odd roll, then Wilkeson was busy assisting other units. If this scenario is played in conjunction with the "Barlow's Knoll" scenario, this rule does not apply, as Wilkeson's Battery is actually deployed in the battle space.

ROCK CREEK

Rock Creek is treated as one inch of heavy woods for infantry or cavalry movement and one inch of rough terrain for artillery movement. Infantry in or crossing Rock Creek are in disorder. If an infantry or cavalry unit attempts to fire while in Rock Creek, it suffers an extra -4 DRM firing detriment to all its fires. Artillery may not fire while in Rock Creek. If a unit is targeted while in Rock Creek, the firer gets an extra +4 DRM firing benefit. (For further details and photo, see Gettysburg terrain descriptions.)

WOODS

All wooded areas are defined as light woods.

RIDGE CREST LINE

The slopes on the ridge in the center of the game board are gentle and rolling. The crest of that ridge line is marked by the indicated fence line. Any unit that is within an inch of the fence marking the crest line is high enough on the hill to see over the crest line to the other side.

SUMMARY ORDER OF BATTLE
(For brigade, regiment and battery details see Army List)

THE UNION FORCES

Devin's Cavalry Brigade – 2nd Brigade/1st Cavalry Division – Colonel Thomas Devin (1 LB)
   At start, 2 p.m. scenario only
XI Corps – Two regiments of Von Gilsa's Brigade
   At start
- 54th New York
- 153rd Philadelphia

XII Corps / 1st Division – Brigadier General Alpheus Williams (1 LB)
- McDougall's -1st Brigade – Colonel Archibald McDougall (1 LB) – Arrives 2 p.m.
- Ruger's- 3rd Brigade – Brigadier General Thomas Ruger (1 LB) – Arrives 3 p.m.
- Lockwood's – 2nd Brigade – Brigadier General Harry Lockwood (1 LB) – Arrives 4 p.m.

XII Corps Artillery Brigade – Lieutenant Edward D. Muhlenberg (no LB)
   Arrives 2.30 p.m.
- Winegar's Battery
- Atwell's Battery
- Rugg's Battery
- Kinzie's Battery

THE CONFEDERATE FORCES

II Corps / Early's Division – Major General Jubal Early (1 LB)
- Gordon's Brigade – Brigadier General John Gordon (2 LB)
- Hays' Brigade – Brigadier General Harry Hays (1 LB)
- Hoke's Brigade – Colonel Isaac Avery (1 LB) – Arrives at 3 p.m.
- Smith's Brigade – Brigadier General William "Extra Billy" Smith (no LB) – Arrives at 4 p.m.

Early's Divisional Artillery Battalion – Lieutenant Colonel Hillary P. Jones (No Artillery LB)
   Arrives at 2 p.m.
- Green's Battery, Garber's Battery, Tanner's Battery, Carrington's Battery
- 17th Virginia Cavalry (From Jenkins' Brigade – see special rules)

A LONG AFTERNOON, A VERY LONG DAY, A VERY TOUGH DAY

A LONG AFTERNOON
2 p.m. to 6 p.m., July 1, 1863 – North and West of Gettysburg

The "A Long Afternoon" scenario combines all three of the first day Gettysburg boards and recreates the fighting from 2 p.m. to 6 p.m. In 15mm, this ADF scenario takes up roughly a 5 foot by 9 foot table space, which may suggest that this combined scenario is probably more suited to a convention or a large club game than a smaller venue. The game combines the three scenarios of "McPherson's Ridge," "Barlow's Knoll," and the 2 p.m. version of "Slocum Arrives." The 2 p.m. start time was selected as that was when, after a two-hour lull of nothing more than artillery exchanges, the Confederates would make a concerted assault across the entire front. Heth and Pender's divisions would take the lead in the west along the Chambersburg Pike,

Rodes' Division would attack from the north and Early's Division would attack from the northeast. The one departure from actual events is the presence of the First Division of Slocum's XII Corps from the "Slocum Arrives" scenario. However, should you wish to play it purely as a historical scenario, then the only Union troops that will contest Early's powerful Confederate division will be Devin's dismounted cavalry brigade.

VICTORY CONDITIONS
For the Confederates to win the combined three-board scenario, they must meet the victory conditions of the "Barlow's Knoll" scenario and either the Confederate 5 p.m. victory condition of "McPherson's Ridge" or the Confederate victory condition of the 2 p.m. version of "Slocum Arrives." For the Union to win, they must meet the Union victory condition of any of the two above listed scenarios.

The day began with Buford's cavalry screening the approaches to Gettysburg. (Patrick LeBeau & Chris Ward)

ORDERS OF BATTLE

The Orders of Battle would be as defined as listed in the individual scenarios, and the "linked" starting positions are indicated on the two-page spread that follows. The possible "what if" options include having Major General Edward Johnson's Confederate division coming in behind Major General Robert Rodes' division, and allowing most of Major General Daniel Sickles' III Corps to respond earlier than Sickles historically did, immediately marching to the aid the hard-pressed I Corps after receiving

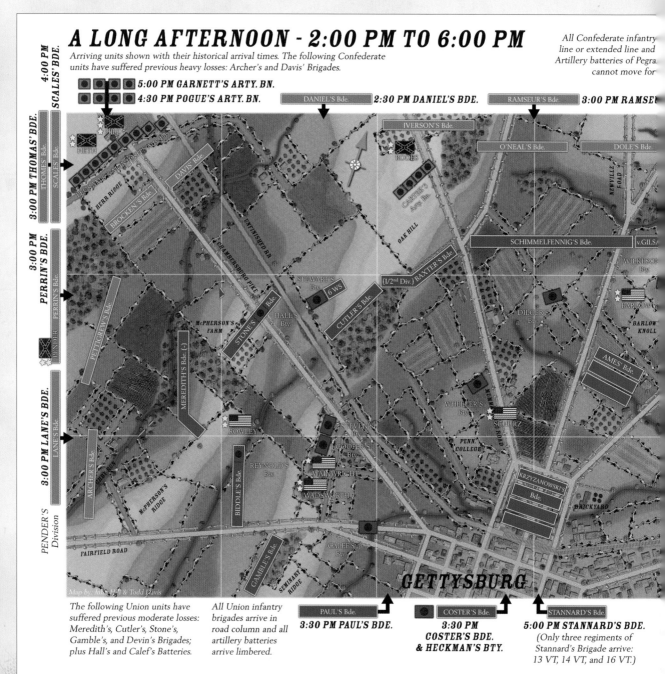

A LONG AFTERNOON - 2:00 PM TO 6:00 PM

Arriving units shown with their historical arrival times. The following Confederate units have suffered previous heavy losses: Archer's and Davis' Brigades.

All Confederate infantry line or extended line and Artillery batteries of Pegra cannot move for

4:00 PM SCALES' BDE.

5:00 PM GARNETT'S ARTY. BN.

4:30 PM POGUE'S ARTY. BN.

2:30 PM DANIEL'S BDE. — DANIEL'S Bde.

3:00 PM RAMSEU — RAMSEUR'S Bde.

3:00 PM THOMAS' BDE. — THOMAS' Bde. / SCALES' Bde.

IVERSON'S Bde.

O'NEAL'S Bde.

DOLE'S Bde.

RODES

CARTER'S Arty. Bn.

3:00 PM PERRIN'S BDE. — PERRIN'S Bde.

OAK HILL

SCHIMMELFENNIG'S Bde.

v. GILS

BROCKEN'S Bde.

DAVIS Bde.

HERR RIDGE

UNFINISHED RR

CHAMBERSBURG PIKE

STEWART'S

6 WS

(1/2nd Div.) BAXTER'S Bde.

WILKESON Bty.

PENDER

PETTIGREW'S Bde.

McPHERSON'S FARM

STONE'S Bde.

HALL'S Bty.

CUTLER'S Bde.

DILGER'S Bty.

BARLOW

BARLOW KNOLL

3:00 PM LANE'S BDE. — LANE'S Bde.

MEREDITH'S Bde. (-)

AMES' Bde.

ARCHER'S Bde.

ROWLEY

STEVEN'S Bty.

COOPER'S Bty.

WHEELER'S Bty.

SCHURZ

PENDER'S Division

McPHERSON'S RIDGE

REYNOLD'S Bty.

BIDDLE'S Bde.

WAINWRIGHT

WADSWORTH

PENN. COLLEGE

KRZYZANOWSKI'S Bde.

BRICKYARD

FAIRFIELD ROAD

GAMBLE'S Bde.

SEMINARY RIDGE

CALEF'S Bty.

GETTYSBURG

Map by: John Hill & Todd Davis

The following Union units have suffered previous moderate losses: Meredith's, Cutler's, Stone's, Gamble's, and Devin's Brigades; plus Hall's and Calef's Batteries.

All Union infantry brigades arrive in road column and all artillery batteries arrive limbered.

PAUL'S Bde.

3:30 PM PAUL'S BDE.

COSTER'S Bde.

3:30 PM COSTER'S BDE. & HECKMAN'S BTY.

STANNARD'S Bde.

5:00 PM STANNARD'S BDE.

(Only three regiments of Stannard's Brigade arrive: 13 VT, 14 VT, and 16 VT.)

Reynolds' request. As was noted earlier, these were very real possibilities. The first one simply required better route-planning on the part of General Ewell's staff, and the second assumes that Sickles does what he actually did, but earlier.

arrive deployed in
es arrive limbered.
cIntosh's Arty. Bns.
4:00 PM.

4:00 PM SMITH'S BDE. — SMITH'S Bde.

3:00 PM HOKE'S BDE. — HOKE'S Bde.

2:30 PM HAYS' BDE. — HAY'S Bde.

2:00 PM GORDON'S BDE. — 2:00 PM JONES' ARTY. BN. / GORDON'S Bde. / EARLY

153 PA

5 NY Reg

9 NY Reg

27 PA Reg

54 NY

XII Corps units

HEIDLESBURG ROAD

RIDGE CREST LINE

DEVIN'S CAVALRY BRIGADE

HUNTERSTOWN ROAD

RAILROAD

YORK PIKE / HOSPITAL WOODS

WOLF'S HILL

00 PM McDOUGALL'S BDE. — McDOUGALL'S Bde.

PM XII CORPS ARTY. BDE.

3:00 PM RUGER'S BDE. — RUGER'S Bde.

:00 PM LOCKWOOD'S BDE. — LOCKWOOD'S Bde.

1ST DIV./ XII CORPS
Brig. Gen. Alpheus Williams arrives with the XII Corps Arty. Bde.

WILLIAMS

There are other options. If Edward Johnson's division did follow Rodes' division down from Carlisle rather than interposing in front of Major General Richard Anderson's division on the Chambersburg Pike, then Anderson's division could have been up in time on Herr Ridge for a late intervention in the battle, although given Lee's determination to hold Anderson's division in reserve against the unexpected his intervention should be as most unlikely. Likewise, the Second Division of the XII Corps under Brigadier General John Geary could be available, but it had been diverted to secure the Round Tops on the evening of July 1, and it is also most unlikely that the Union would left that position uncovered, as a day earlier Buford had tangled with Confederate infantry and a battery along the Fairfield Road. However, should a game master decide to make these units available, their details are presented in the Army List.

A VERY LONG DAY

8 a.m. to 6 p.m., July 1, 1863 – North and West of Gettysburg

This scenario recreates the entire chronology of the first day of Gettysburg from 8 a.m. to 6 p.m. and is more than just a combination of all the individual scenarios run consecutively. It is a depiction of time lost and opportunities squandered. The illustrated unit arrivals are when the units actually arrived and could have been available for offensive operations. This version of the "First Day" removes some of the historical restraints that the commanders were operating under. In other instances, it starts the clock just before a tactical mistake or oversight was historically made, so that the wargamer is not forced to replicate that same mistake. One of the more useful functions of a wargame is to investigate the impact of alternate decisions while maintaining the overall command and mission context of the situation, and this is the objective of "A Very Long Day."

THE CONFEDERATE SITUATION

The overriding context for the Confederate commanders was Lee's desire not to bring on a general engagement until his army was concentrated and he knew exactly how much of the Army of the Potomac he was facing. This uncertainty led to a command climate of excessive caution that discouraged the Confederate corps and division commanders from using the time and numerical advantage that the situation offered them. The main departure that this scenario takes from history is that

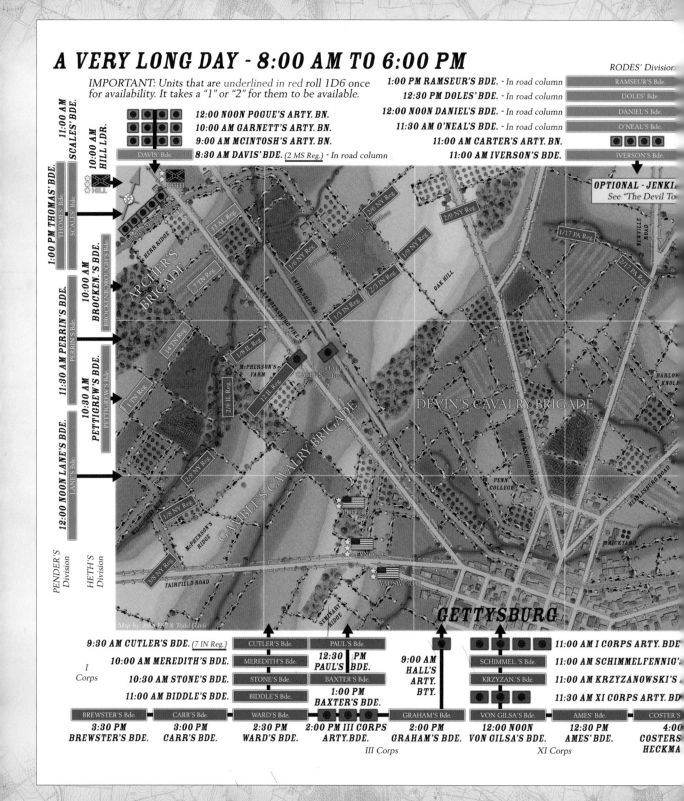

A VERY LONG DAY - 8:00 AM TO 6:00 PM

IMPORTANT: Units that are underlined in red roll 1D6 once for availability. It takes a "1" or "2" for them to be available.

12:00 NOON POGUE'S ARTY. BN.
10:00 AM GARNETT'S ARTY. BN.
9:00 AM MCINTOSH'S ARTY. BN.
8:30 AM DAVIS' BDE. (2 MS Reg.) - In road column

1:00 PM RAMSEUR'S BDE. - In road column
12:30 PM DOLES' BDE. - In road column
12:00 NOON DANIEL'S BDE. - In road column
11:30 AM O'NEAL'S BDE. - In road column
11:00 AM CARTER'S ARTY. BN.
11:00 AM IVERSON'S BDE.

RODES' Division

RAMSEUR'S Bde.
DOLES' Bde.
DANIEL'S Bde.
O'NEAL'S Bde.

IVERSON'S Bde.

OPTIONAL - JENKI
See "The Devil To

11:00 AM SCALES' BDE.
10:00 AM HILL LDR.
1:00 PM THOMAS' BDE.   THOMAS' Bde.   SCALES' Bde.
10:00 AM BROCKEN.'S BDE.   BROCKENBROUGH'S Bde.
11:30 AM PERRIN'S BDE.   PERRIN'S Bde.
10:30 AM PETTIGREW'S BDE.   PETTIGREW'S Bde.
12:00 NOON LANE'S BDE.   LANE'S Bde.

DAVIS' Bde.

PENDER'S Division
HETH'S Division

ARCHER'S BRIGADE

GAMBLE'S CAVALRY BRIGADE
DEVIN'S CAVALRY BRIGADE

McPHERSON'S FARM
CALEF'S Bty.
HALL'S Bty.
McPHERSON'S RIDGE

OAK HILL

BARLOW KNOLL

PENN. COLLEGE

BRICKYARD

BUFORD
REYNOLDS
WADSWORTH

SEMINARY RIDGE

FAIRFIELD ROAD

GETTYSBURG

NEWVILLE ROAD
HEMLESBURG ROAD

Map by: John Hill & Todd Davis

9:30 AM CUTLER'S BDE. (7 IN Reg.)   CUTLER'S Bde.   PAUL'S Bde.   11:00 AM I CORPS ARTY. BDE
10:00 AM MEREDITH'S BDE.   MEREDITH'S Bde.   12:30 PM PAUL'S BDE.   SCHIMMEL.'S Bde.   11:00 AM SCHIMMELFENNIG'
10:30 AM STONE'S BDE.   STONE'S Bde.   BAXTER'S Bde.   9:00 AM HALL'S ARTY. BTY.   KRZYZAN.'S Bde.   11:00 AM KRZYZANOWSKI'S
11:00 AM BIDDLE'S BDE.   BIDDLE'S Bde.   1:00 PM BAXTER'S BDE.   11:30 AM XI CORPS ARTY. BD

I Corps

BREWSTER'S Bde.   CARR'S Bde.   WARD'S Bde.   GRAHAM'S Bde.   VON GILSA'S Bde.   AMES' Bde.   COSTER'S
3:30 PM BREWSTER'S BDE.   3:00 PM CARR'S BDE.   2:30 PM WARD'S BDE.   2:00 PM III CORPS ARTY.BDE.   2:00 PM GRAHAM'S BDE.   12:00 NOON VON GILSA'S BDE.   12:30 PM AMES' BDE.   4:00 COSTERS HECKMA

III Corps

XI Corps

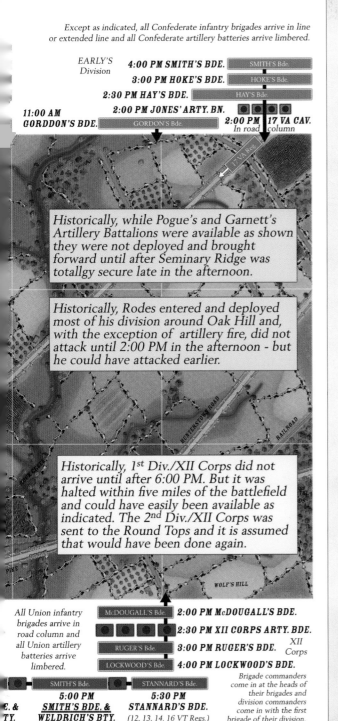

Except as indicated, all Confederate infantry brigades arrive in line or extended line and all Confederate artillery batteries arrive limbered.

EARLY'S Division

4:00 PM SMITH'S BDE. — SMITH'S Bde.

3:00 PM HOKE'S BDE. — HOKE'S Bde.

2:30 PM HAY'S BDE. — HAY'S Bde.

2:00 PM JONES' ARTY. BN.

11:00 AM GORDDON'S BDE. — GORDON'S Bde.

2:00 PM 17 VA CAV. In road column

Historically, while Pogue's and Garnett's Artillery Battalions were available as shown they were not deployed and brought forward until after Seminary Ridge was totallgy secure late in the afternoon.

Historically, Rodes entered and deployed most of his division around Oak Hill and, with the exception of artillery fire, did not attack until 2:00 PM in the afternoon - but he could have attacked earlier.

Historically, 1st Div./XII Corps did not arrive until after 6:00 PM. But it was halted within five miles of the battlefield and could have easily been available as indicated. The 2nd Div./XII Corps was sent to the Round Tops and it is assumed that would have been done again.

WOLF'S HILL

All Union infantry brigades arrive in road column and all Union artillery batteries arrive limbered.

McDOUGALL'S Bde. — 2:00 PM McDOUGALL'S BDE.

2:30 PM XII CORPS ARTY. BDE.

RUGER'S Bde. — 3:00 PM RUGER'S BDE. — XII Corps

LOCKWOOD'S Bde. — 4:00 PM LOCKWOOD'S BDE.

SMITH'S Bde. — STANNARD'S Bde.

5:00 PM SMITH'S BDE. & WELDRICH'S BTY.

5:30 PM STANNARD'S BDE. (12, 13, 14, 16 VT Regs.)

Brigade commanders come in at the heads of their brigades and division commanders come in with the first brigade of their division.

there is no lull from 12 noon to 2 p.m. when the only Confederate activity was artillery shelling. In ADF, that would be four turns of no Confederate attacks, which would drive most wargamers crazy. The shorter "A Long Afternoon" scenario takes the historical lull into account by not starting the scenario until 2 p.m. The other historical departure for this version of "First Day" is letting the Confederates use some but not all of their III Corps units that were available. This would include Garnett's and Pogue's artillery battalions and Thomas' Infantry Brigade. Lee, however, on July 1 was determined to keep Anderson III Corps division and Johnson's II Corps division in reserve against any unexpected eventuality, and this scenario maintains that understandable restriction.

Historically, as Robert Rodes and his division arrived from Carlisle they were in a perfect position to immediately drive towards Gettysburg and roll up the Union XI Corps as it arrived, and perhaps to cut off the retreat of the Union I Corps. Instead, Rodes would take two hours to move his division closer to Oak Hill – admittedly, a very good position – and take the time to set up a flank attack on the Union I Corps. Ironically, two of his brigade commanders, generals Iverson and O'Neal, would bungle that attack and almost negate Rodes' careful preparations. This scenario put Rodes in his historically correct arrival position, but does not force him to redeploy his division towards Oak Hill and wait two hours before attacking.

THE UNION SITUATION

Unlike Lee, General George Meade had a fairly good idea of where all of Lee's elements were located and what they were doing. His chief intelligence officer, Colonel George H. Sharp, was able to provide Meade with updated information on the Army of Northern Virginia that was consistently accurate by making use of all information sources. Though General Meade knew that Lee's army was very spread out, he still had a healthy respect for the generalship of his opponent. Consequently, he was torn between two basic concepts of operation. One concept was to have his seven corps advance as rapidly as possible and to pitch into Lee – in whatever order they arrived – before Lee could fully concentrate his army. The other option was to concentrate his own army in a strong position between the Confederates and Washington and wait for Lee to attack him. The result was an unintentional compromise, with Reynolds' left wing moving forward to engage as quickly as possible, and the other corps holding back in anticipation of an eventual defensive fight along Pipe Creek. This version of the "First Day" also assumes, as does the "A Long Afternoon" scenario, that Slocum sends William's first division north earlier than it was actually done. But it also looks at the effect of the Pipe Creek circular on III Corps.

Daniel Sickles' III Corps was a victim of conflicting orders. Around noon, General Sickles had received General Reynolds' last message, saying that "he had better come up," and since Reynolds was the left wing commander, that was a legal order. However, the army commander General Meade had previously ordered III Corps to stay put at Emmitsburg to secure the left flank of the Pipe Creek line. General Sickles continued to dither until about 3 p.m. when he received General Howard's message that "General Reynolds is dead, for God's sake come up." At that point, General Sickles decided to respond and after leaving two brigades and two batteries at Emmitsburg, he began moving the rest of III Corps up to Gettysburg. This variant assumes that Sickles does exactly as he did, but does it immediately upon receiving General Reynolds' request for help rather than up to three hours later. In that case, most of III Corps – with the exception of De Trobriand's and Burling's Brigade along with Winslow's and Smith's batteries – could begin arriving at Gettysburg at about 2 p.m. and are included in the "A Very Long Day" scenario. Ironically, that night Meade approved of Sickles' decision and ordered him also to bring up the remaining two brigades and two batteries that had been left behind at Emmitsburg.

A VERY TOUGH DAY
8 a.m. to 6 p.m., July 1, 1863 – North and West of Gettysburg

This scenario is an optional addition to "A Very Long Day." It uses all the units portrayed in that scenario, plus the additional units that both sides could have had available with better pre-battle planning. If the Confederates had paid more attention to how their forces approached Gettysburg and the route capacity of the roads, they could have had both Johnson's and Anderson's divisions available that afternoon. For the Union, had not the Pipe Creek Circular created some confusion as to General Meade's intent, then all of III Corps and XII Corps would have arrived in time to stiffen the defense. The additional units that this option offers assumes "the best that each side could do," and though the net effect will heavily favor the Confederates, this it could still be a good scenario if the Confederate players are less experienced than the Union players.

CONFEDERATE ALTERNATE SITUATION
Edward Johnson's and Richard Anderson's divisions were victims of poor administration at General Ewell's II Corps headquarters. When General Lee cancelled Ewell's planned attack on Harrisburg and instead ordered the Army to concentrate at Chambersburg, Johnston was ordered to immediately proceed to Chambersburg. Lee, however, then modified his orders and directed II Corps to concentrate at Gettysburg or Cashtown. However, Ewell or his staff did not send new orders to Johnson to counter-march and follow Rodes' Division down to Gettysburg, thereby keeping the II Corps together. Instead, Johnson would proceed to interpose into III Corps' line of march in front of Anderson's Division, causing a monumental traffic jam on the Chambersburg Pike. This delayed Anderson's Division and in turn Longstreet's entire corps, in addition to Johnson's Division. This scenario assumes that Ewell's staff was paying attention to such details and did indeed order Johnson's Division to counter-march so as to be in position to follow Rodes' Division into Gettysburg. This variant of the "First Day" also assumes that Lee overcomes his uncharacteristic caution and reverts to his normal style of bold aggressive actions and allows most of Johnson's and Anderson's divisions to join the offensive as soon as they are deployed. However, Lee, still being unsure of where the rest of the Union Army was, would probably have kept a brigade back from each division along with the II Corps Reserve Artillery as a reserve.

UNION RESPONSE
Faced with the escalating Confederate aggressiveness, it is assumed that the Union would make use of all troops that were close at hand. This would be the remainder of Slocum's XII Corps and the rest of Sickle's III Corps. Other major Union units, such as Major General Winfield Hancock's II Corps and Major General George Sykes' V Corps, would still be too far away to make a difference until the morning of July 2. If on that "First Day" the Union had been forced to contend with all of Ewell's II Corps and all of A. P. Hill's III Corps, it is very likely that General Meade would have activated his plan to fall back and defend along Pipe Creek.

VICTORY CONDITIONS
Since the availability and release of Anderson's and Johnson's divisions will tilt the battle in favor of the Confederates, they must meet all the victory conditions of "Seminary Ridge," "Barlow's Knoll" and "Slocum Arrives." For the Union to win, they have to prevent the Confederates from meeting all three of the victory conditions for those scenarios.

"A VERY TOUGH DAY"

II CORPS/ JOHNSON'S DIVISION
Steuart's Brigade and the III Corps Reserve Artillery would be kept in reserve.

4:00 PM NICHOL'S BDE.
NICHOL'S Bde.

3:30 PM JONES' BDE.
JONES' Bde.

3:30 PM LATIMER'S ARTY. BN.
enters limbered

3:30 PM LANE'S ARTY. BN.
Roll 1D6 by battery: takes 1 or 2 for release; batteries enter limbered.
(Ross', Patterson's, & Wingfield's Batteries.)

All Confederate infantry brigades arrive deployed in line or extended line.

3:00 PM WALKER'S BDE.
JOHNSON   WALKER'S Bde.

4:00 PM WRIGHT'S BDE.
WRIGHT'S Bde.

3:30 PM WILCOX'S BDE.
WILCOX'S Bde.

ANDERSON

4:00 PM POSEY'S BDE.
POSEY'S Bde.

3:30 PM MAHONE'S BDE.
MAHONE'S Bde.

III CORPS/ANDERSON'S DIVISION - Perry's Brigade and some of Lane's Arty. Bn. would be kept in reserve.

HERR RIDGE

UNFINISHED RR.

CHAMBERSBURG PIKE

OAK HILL

CARLISLE ROAD

NEWVILLE ROAD

McPHERSON'S FARM

BARLOW'S KNOLL

MUMMASBURG ROAD

PENN COLLEGE

BRICKYARD

WILLOUGHBY

McPHERSON'S RIDGE

FAIRFIELD ROAD

SEMINARY RIDGE

GETTYSBURG

REMAINDER OF UNION III CORPS FROM EMMITSBURG:

4:00 PM De TROBRIANDS BDE. & SMITH'S BTY.
De TROBRIAND'S Bde.

4:30 PM BURLING'S BDE. & WINSLOW'S BTY.
BURLING'S Bde.

CANDY'S Bde.
COBHAM'S Bde.
GREEN'S Bde.

GEARY

3:00 PM CANDY'S BDE.

3:30 PM COBHAM'S BDE.

4:00 PM GREEN'S BDE.

2ND DIV./ XII CORPS

All Union infantry brigades arrive in road column and all Union batteries arrive limbered.

ATTACKING THE PIPE CREEK LINE

Early Morning, July 1, 1863

"If the enemy assumes the offensive and attacks, it is the intention, after holding them in check sufficiently long … to withdraw the army from its present position and form line of battle, with the left resting on Middleburg and the right at Manchester, with the general direction being that of Pipe Creek." – The Pipe Creek Circular

In the early hours of July 1, General George Meade's staff had finally completed making all the required copies of the 20-paragraph Pipe Creek Circular that was to be sent to all his corps commanders. Meade was incensed that it took so long and was heard to grumble that getting it out took so long – the better part of a day – that it "was now useless." The document outlined in detail what may have been General Meade's preferred battle scheme – a defensive engagement along Pipe Creek. Almost certainly, the most important person in

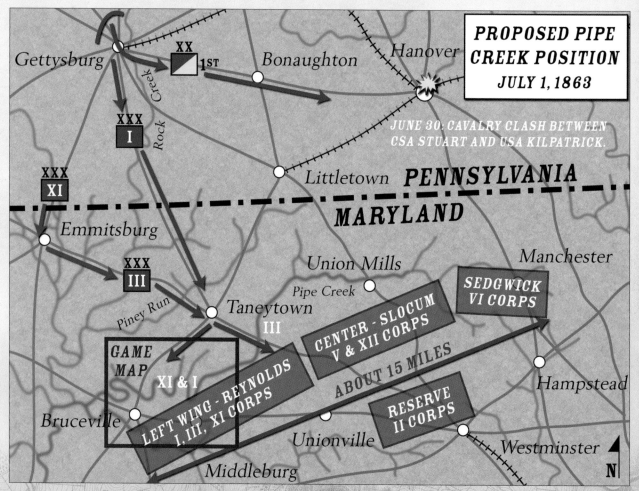

PROPOSED PIPE CREEK POSITION JULY 1, 1863

JUNE 30: CAVALRY CLASH BETWEEN CSA STUART AND USA KILPATRICK.

this plan was that of Major General John Reynolds, who as the left wing commander would be directing the three corps – the First, the Third, and the Eleventh – that would most likely be the first units to meet the advancing Confederates now known to be heading toward Gettysburg. As events unfolded, Reynolds, being true to his combative nature, would pitch into the Confederates as far forward as possible and would delay their advance long enough to define Gettysburg as the place where the battle would be fought. However, somewhere in northern Maryland or southern Pennsylvania, the courier carrying Reynolds' copy of the Pipe Creek Circular was hopelessly lost, and consequently Reynolds would never see Meade's concept of operation, which had his three-corps "wing" holding the critical left flank of the Pipe Creek Line. Had that courier actually found Reynolds and made him aware of Meade's preferred defensive option, Reynolds might not have pushed his forces that far forward and instead may have fought a delaying action at Gettysburg, in anticipation of Meade issuing the execution order for the Army to concentrate along Pipe Creek as most of the other generals expected him to. This is the basis for this campaign scenario: Reynolds does receive his copy of the Pipe Creek Circular, Meade gives the implementation order, and events take a different turn.

MIDMORNING, SEMINARY RIDGE

By late morning, it had become obvious to General A. P. Hill that the Union defense north of Gettysburg had been a skilful delaying action by Federal cavalry and a few of brigades of infantry. Although the fighting had left General Henry Heth somewhat confused, it was now apparent that the lead elements of the Army of the Potomac were falling back to a different defensive position. The fight would not be here. Though the Army of Northern Virginia was not fully concentrated, his leading III Corps – particularly with Johnson's II Corps division in the middle of it – was probably strong enough to continue to press the Federals before they could become concentrated on a battlefield of their choice. Sending Johnson's division into the middle of his line march had been a mistake, but that mistake could perhaps be turned into an opportunity, as it now gave Hill's III corps substantial additional offensive power. He quickly wrote out a message for Lee, advising that the Federals were retreating and that an aggressive pursuit might defeat a large element of the Federal Army before it could concentrate. As Pegram's Battalion relimbered its guns and Heth's Division reformed into march columns, Hill received Lee's reply, "By all means, push those people. Longstreet and Ewell will follow. You may use Johnson's Division until Ewell is up. Any word from Stuart?"

The Confederates arrive at the new Union position and deploy overlooking Pipe Creek. (Patrick LeBeau & Chris Ward)

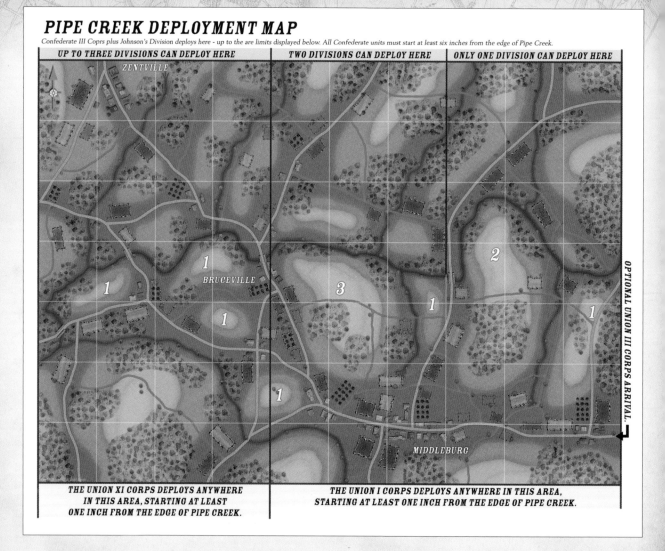

PIPE CREEK DEPLOYMENT MAP

Confederate III Coprs plus Johnson's Division deploys here - up to the are limits displayed below. All Confederate units must start at least six inches from the edge of Pipe Creek.

| UP TO THREE DIVISIONS CAN DEPLOY HERE | TWO DIVISIONS CAN DEPLOY HERE | ONLY ONE DIVISION CAN DEPLOY HERE |

ZENTVILLE

BRUCEVILLE

MIDDLEBURG

OPTIONAL UNION III CORPS ARRIVAL.

THE UNION XI CORPS DEPLOYS ANYWHERE
IN THIS AREA, STARTING AT LEAST
ONE INCH FROM THE EDGE OF PIPE CREEK.

THE UNION I CORPS DEPLOYS ANYWHERE IN THIS AREA,
STARTING AT LEAST ONE INCH FROM THE EDGE OF PIPE CREEK.

JULY 1: THE PIPE CREEK UNION DEPLOYMENT

The Pipe Creek Circular defined the intended final dispositions as shown. For this mini-campaign scenario, it is assumed that the execution order has the III Corps moving first through Taneytown and eventually joining the II Corps as a reserve around Unionville. After the III Corps cleared Taneytown, the XI and I Corps would move to the Bruceville-Middleburg area. Historically, there was a cavalry clash at Hanover on June 30, and it is assumed that Buford's 1st Cavalry Division would be ordered to that area in case that cavalry battle escalated. The probable left wing deployment would have the XI

Corps on the left and the I Corps on the right, with the III Corps at Unionville in a position to assist Reynolds on the left or Slocum in the center, depending on where the pursuing Confederates might make their main attack.

JULY 1: THE CONFEDERATE ATTACK

It will be assumed that the first elements of A. P. Hill's III Corps would have started arriving in the area sometime after 11 a.m. and could have been deployed for the attack by 1 p.m. with the bulk of the III corps in the Zentville area, but only one division could have made it all the way over to the his east flank per the deployment area map. It is assumed that Lee would have allowed A. P. Hill to temporarily retain Johnson's division for the attack, but the II Corps Artillery Reserve would probably be held back at Gettysburg until it could re-join the II Corps divisions coming down from Carlisle and York.

A MODERATED SCENARIO
This scenario should be a moderated mini-campaign game, as the battle space is far too big for any one gameboard. It is recommended that this be a team game, with each side "deploying" and recording their forces on a copy of the entire battle space. These copies are then turned over to the moderator, who will decide how to set up the actual gaming table based on their recorded deployments and any special orders that the respective commanders may have for their units. At that point, the moderator has control of the game. He can decide if and when any Union III Corps units are brought in from their reserve position at Uniontown and whether General Lee lets A. P. Hill use the II Corps reserve artillery or not. Though the map does not show fences or walls, they would certainly be integral to the farm areas and will be placed by the moderator. The moderator also has the option of deciding who will have the initiative, and modifying any of the terrain or the network of farm roads as period maps were usually incomplete and often inaccurate. The battle is considered to be over by 6 p.m. or as late as 8 p.m. depending on the moderator's decision. Victory in this mini-campaign game is determined by occupying critical "point value" locations by the end of the game, with victory going to the side with the most points. If both sides have equal points, the game is a draw.

SUMMARY ORDER OF BATTLE
(For brigade, regiment and battery details see Army List)

ARMY OF THE POTOMAC LEFT WING: MAJOR GENERAL JOHN REYNOLDS

I Corps: Major General John Reynolds (14,000 men, 28 guns)
I Corps: 1st Division (James Wadsworth)
• Meredith's Brigade
• Cutler's Brigade

I Corps: 2nd Division (John Robinson)
• Paul's Brigade
• Baxter's Brigade

I Corps: 3rd Division (Thomas Rowley)
• Biddle's Brigade
• Stone's Brigade
• Stannard's Brigade

I Corps Artillery Brigade (Charles Wainwright)

XI Corps: Major General Oliver Otis Howard (10,800 men, 26 guns)
XI Corps: 1st Division (Francis Barlow)
• Von Gilsa's Brigade
• Ames' Brigade

XI Corps: 2nd Division (Adolph von Steinwehr)
• Coster's Brigade
• Smith's Brigade

XI Corps: 3rd Division (Carl Schurz)
• Schimmelfennig's Brigade
• Krzyzanowski's Brigade

XI Corps Artillery Brigade (Thomas Osborne)

III Corps: Major General Daniel Sickles (13,000 men, 30 guns)
   Moderator Option: Late Arrival – either entire corps or by individual divisions.
III Corps: 1st Division (David Birney)
• Graham's Brigade
• Ward's Brigade
• Regis de Trobriand's Brigade

III Corps: 2nd Division (Andrew Humphreys)
• Carr's Brigade
• Brewster's Brigade
• Burling's Brigade

III Corps Artillery Brigade (George Randolph)

ARMY OF NORTHERN VIRGINIA

III Corps: Major General A. P. Hill (23,000 men, 84 guns)

Heth's Division (Henry Heth)
- Archer's Brigade
- Davis' Brigade
- Pettigrew's Brigade
- Brockenbrough's Brigade
- Garnett's Artillery Battalion

Pender's Division (W. D. Pender)
- McGowan's Brigade
- Lane's Brigade
- Scales' Brigade
- Thomas' Brigade
- Pogue's Artillery Battalion

Anderson's Division (Richard Anderson)
- Wilcox's Brigade
- Perry's Brigade
- Wright's Brigade
- Posey's Brigade
- Mahone's Brigade
- Lane's Artillery Battalion

III Corps Reserve Artillery (R. L. Walker)
- Pegram's Artillery Battalion
- McIntosh's Artillery Battalion

Temporarily Attached (6,400 men, 16 guns)
II Corps, Johnson's Division (E. Johnson)
- Steuart's Brigade
- Nichols' Brigade
- Walker's Brigade
- Jones' Brigade
- Snowden's Artillery Battalion

II Corps Reserve Artillery (T. T. Brown) (31 guns)
  Moderator Option
- Dance's Artillery Battalion
- Nelsen's Artillery Battalion

ATTACKING THE PIPE CREEK LINE – SMALL VERSION

This version of the Battle at Pipe Creek, which does not require a moderator, uses some slightly different assumptions. For the Confederates, it assumes that Lee decides to hold Johnson's Division and the II Corps back at Gettysburg so that they can reunite with the rest of Ewell's II Corps. For the Union, it assumes that III Corps departed from Emmitsburg as before and continued to go into reserve at Unionville. Meanwhile, XI Corps under Howard was slow off the mark in pulling back – claiming that he was held up by the III Corps trains – and by the time he would was ready to turn towards Taneytown, the Confederates were already approaching it. So, after some confusion, Howard will bring the XI Corps to the Pipe Creek position by a longer but safer back route. His XI Corps will begin arriving in one long march column as indicated on the west edge at the start of the 12.30 p.m. turn.

SCENARIO TIME AND VICTORY CONDITIONS

This scenario starts at 12 noon and goes to the end of the 5 p.m. turn. As in the larger scenario, the side holding the terrain with the most victory points at the end of the scenario wins, but note that for this scenario, the terrain victory points are somewhat different.

SCENARIO INITIATIVE

Since the Confederates are on the offensive, it is assumed that they have the initiative throughout the scenario. However, if the III Corps commander Major General A. P. Hill is killed, then the initiative shifts to the Union beginning with the next turn. If the Union commander Major General John Reynolds is killed, then the initiative is permanently with the Confederates regardless of whether A.P. Hill is alive or dead.

PIPE CREEK DEPLOYMENT MAP - SMALL VERSION

III Corps arrival area - all units enter in road column or as skirmishers at 12:00 Noon.

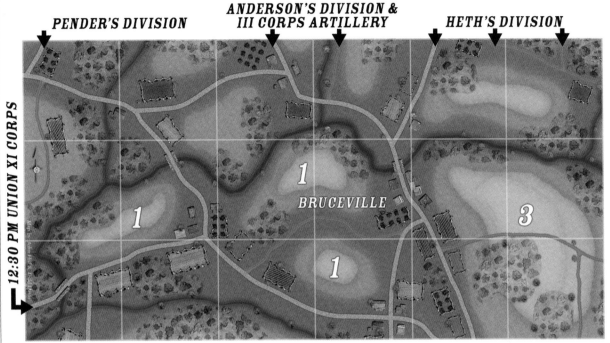

I Corps units start in position anywhere on board up to one inch of the south edge of Pipe Creek. Units deployed in woods are hidden and are revealed when they move or fire. Skirmishers may be deployed across Pipe Creek within four inches of the north edge of Pipe Creek.

"PUT THE BOYS IN!"

The Shenandoah Valley, May 1864, by Dean West

"The Rebs won't gobble us this time!" – Major General Franz Sigel

Lieutenant General U. S Grant's grand plan to win the war in the Eastern Theater called for a spring offensive by four armies. Major General George Meade's massive Army of the Potomac would seek out and destroy Robert E. Lee's Army of Northern Virginia somewhere in the hinterlands along the Rappahannock River. Simultaneously, Major General Benjamin Butler's Army of the James would land at Bermuda Hundred and advance along the James River and threaten Richmond from the south. To support these major offensives, Major General Franz Sigel, commander of the Department of West Virginia, was instructed to organize two smaller armies for offensive operations against Lee's strategic left flank in the vital Shenandoah Valley and south-western Virginia.

One Army was the 9,000-man Army of the Kanawha to be led by Brigadier General George Crook, which would operate out of Charleston, West Virginia. The other would be the 9,000-man Army of the Shenandoah, which Sigel would command himself. Sigel's army would march south from Martinsburg with the primary mission of capturing the Confederate supply base at Staunton. The opening moves of the armies commanded by Meade, Butler and Crook clearly indicate that they fully understood Grant's expectation that the campaign proceed with indomitable offensive spirit. But that sense of aggressive urgency appears to have escaped General Franz Sigel.

Sigel's army marched from Martinsburg on April 29 and ambled south at a slug's pace, which included time off for a "mock battle." It took 16 days for the head of his column, under Colonel Augustus Moor, to reach the outskirts of New Market. Unfortunately for Colonel Moor, numerous detachments to guard against Rebel raiders and frivolous delays had reduced that column to just over 6,000 men. During the afternoon of May 14, just north of New Market, a lively skirmish ensued that continued into the evening and ended with the town still in Confederate hands. Moor took up a defensive position on a ridge just north of the town, knowing that he now faced a sizable Confederate force that appeared ready and eager for battle. As the sun came up and with a battle imminent, Colonel Moor was uneasy and anxiously wondered when the rest of Sigel's scattered army would arrive.

THE CONFEDERATES GATHER

"We can attack and whip them here ... and I'll do it!" – Major General John C. Breckinridge

After learning that the Union Army had once again entered the valley in force, the veteran Confederate leader Major General John C. Breckinridge of Kentucky pulled together all available forces to repulse this latest Federal threat. It would take time for Breckinridge to gather enough units to cobble together a credible defensive force, but Sigel's leisurely advance of fits and start would give him that time. By early May, Breckinridge had assembled a force of approximately 4,000 muskets and 18 guns. The core of his little army was two experienced infantry brigades under brigadier generals John C. Echols and Gabriel C. Wharton, along with a cavalry brigade under the wily Brigadier General John D. Imboden. Filling out his command was a number of smaller battalions, including the untested but eager and well-led 247-man cadet corps of the Virginia Military Institute (VMI).

Breckinridge originally concentrated his force at Staunton, while Imboden and other Confederate cavalry elements harassed Sigel's advance. On May 13, Breckinridge decided to move north and confront Sigel before the Unionist reached Staunton. Breckinridge pushed his advance elements and cavalry to just beyond New Market, while holding his main body in readiness at Lacy Springs. Following the initial May 14 clash with elements of Colonel Moor's "ad hoc" brigade, Breckenridge gave the order for his entire force to move out at 1 a.m. with the hope of surprising and defeating Sigel while much of his army was still straggling southward along the Valley Turnpike. By early morning, Breckinridge had his army massed and ready on high ground just south of New Market.

SCENARIO SPECIFIC RULES

SCENARIO LENGTH, INITIATIVE AND VICTORY CONDITION

The scenario starts with the 11.30 a.m. turn and ends at the conclusion of the 3 p.m. turn for a total game length of seven turns. For the entire scenario the Confederates

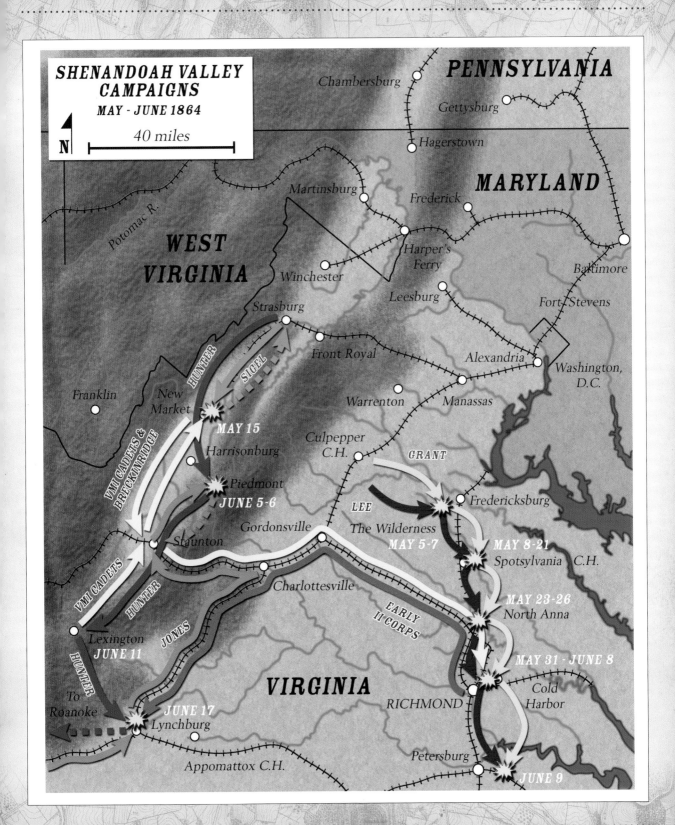

SHENANDOAH VALLEY CAMPAIGNS
MAY – JUNE 1864

N

40 miles

PENNSYLVANIA

Chambersburg

Gettysburg

Hagerstown

MARYLAND

Martinsburg

Frederick

Potomac R.

WEST VIRGINIA

Winchester

Harper's Ferry

Leesburg

Baltimore

Strasburg

Fort Stevens

Front Royal

Alexandria

Washington, D.C.

Franklin

New Market

MAY 15

Warrenton

Manassas

Harrisonburg

Culpepper C.H.

GRANT

Piedmont

JUNE 5-6

Fredericksburg

LEE

The Wilderness

MAY 5-7

Gordonsville

MAY 8-21

Spotsylvania C.H.

Staunton

Charlottesville

MAY 23-26

North Anna

EARLY II CORPS

MAY 31 - JUNE 8

Lexington

JUNE 11

JONES

HUNTER

VMI CADETS

Cold Harbor

RICHMOND

VIRGINIA

To Roanoke

JUNE 17

Lynchburg

Appomattox C.H.

Petersburg

JUNE 9

SIGEL

HUNTER

VMI CADETS & BRECKINRIDGE

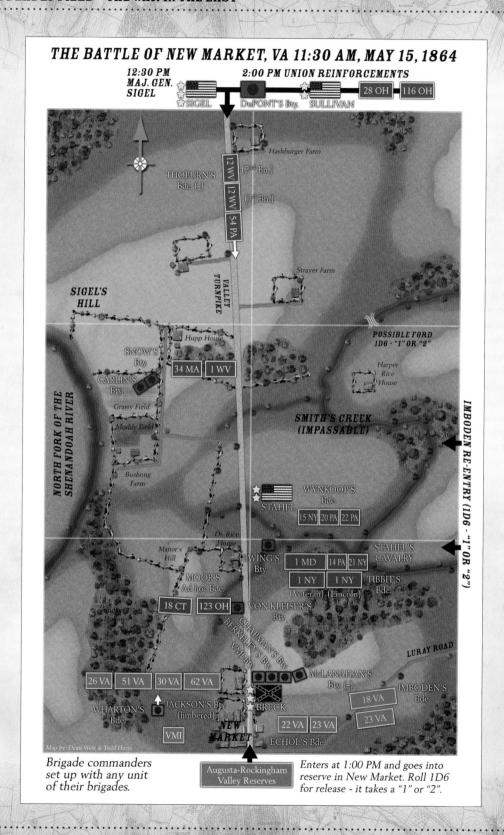

THE BATTLE OF NEW MARKET, VA 11:30 AM, MAY 15, 1864

12:30 PM
MAJ. GEN.
SIGEL

2:00 PM UNION REINFORCEMENTS

SIGEL — DuPONT'S Bty. — SULLIVAN — 28 OH — 116 OH

Hashburger Farm

THOBURN'S Bde. (-)

12 WV (2nd Bn.)
12 WV (1st Bn.)
54 PA

VALLEY TURNPIKE

Strayer Farm

SIGEL'S HILL

POSSIBLE FORD
1D6 - "1" OR "2"

Hupp House

SNOW'S Bty.

CARLIN'S Bty.

34 MA 1 WV

Harper Rice House

NORTH FORK OF THE SHENANDOAH RIVER

Grassy Field

Muddy Field

SMITH'S CREEK
(IMPASSABLE)

Bushong Farm

STAHEL

WYNKOOP'S Bde.

15 NY 20 PA 22 PA

IMBODEN RE-ENTRY (1D6 - "1" OR "2")

Dr. Rice House

Manor's Hill

EWING'S Bty.

1 MD 14 PA 21 NY

1 NY (Veteran) 1 NY (Lincoln)

STAHEL'S CAVALRY

MOOR'S Ad hoc Bde.

TIBBIT'S Bde.

18 CT 123 OH

VON KLEISER'S Bty.

CHAPMAN'S Bty.

BERKELEY'S Bty.

VMI Bty.

LURAY ROAD

26 VA 51 VA 30 VA 62 VA

McLANAHAN'S Bty. (-)

IMBODEN'S Bde.

WHARTON'S Bde.

JACKSON'S Bty. (limbered)

BRECK.

18 VA

VMI

NEW MARKET

22 VA 23 VA

23 VA

ECHOL'S Bde.

Map by: Dean West & Todd Davis

Brigade commanders set up with any unit of their brigades.

Augusta-Rockingham Valley Reserves

Enters at 1:00 PM and goes into reserve in New Market. Roll 1D6 for release - it takes a "1" or "2".

have the initiative. For the Confederates to win, there must be no more than two Union units on the bottom four squares of the game board, and any Union units east of Swift Creek do not count against the Confederate victory conditions. For the Union to win, they must prevent the Confederate victory condition.

TERRAIN DESCRIPTION

All the woods are light woods and the hills are gentle slopes. Since it had been raining, the slopes are somewhat slippery, so if a unit is moving up two or more elevations in one movement action the whole move is done at one movement rate worse. Crossing one or more fences only costs one additional inch of movement, or the whole movement can be made as if it was broken terrain. Normally there would be no extra movement cost to cross the little streams, but since it had been raining it costs one extra inch to cross one or more of them. They have no effect on combat. The escarpment along the Shenandoah River is impassable, as is Smith's Creek, with the possible exception of the one ford. The field designated as "Mud Field" was excessively muddy, and movement through it is done at the light woods rate. When the VMI cadets charged across this field, the mud was so sticky that it sucked many of their shoes off and from then on it has been known as the "field of lost shoes."

POSSIBLE FORD

Despite the heavy rains, the ford across Smith's Creek may be usable. When the first unit comes up to it, roll 1D6, and if a 1 or 2 is rolled, the ford is usable. This one roll determines the status of the ford for the entire scenario. It takes one whole movement action for a unit to use the ford and to cross the creek – from one side to the other – with the movement ending in disorder. Historically, this ford was probably used by Colonel William Boyd of the 1st New York Lincoln Cavalry to retreat after being soundly thrashed on May 13 by Imboden's cavalry.

IMBODEN RE-ENTRY

Imboden's cavalry brigade (18th and 23rd Virginia) and up to one other unit can exit off the east edge of the game board via the Luray Road. Beginning on the next Confederate active turn after these units have left, the Confederate player rolls 1D6 for re-entry and Imboden's command can re-enter on the east edge of the game board where indicated with the roll of a 1 or 2. If a 3, 4, or 5 is rolled, Imboden is still in transit, but the Confederate player can roll again on his next active turn.

However, if a 6 is rolled, the heavy rains have washed out the bridge that Imboden historically used to cross swollen Smith's Creek, and all his units return via the Luray Road on the next Confederate active turn.

VMI CADETS

"We began to learn, much to our regret, that fighting was not as pleasant as we had anticipated." – VMI Cadet John J. Coleman

There was strong reluctance by General Breckinridge to actually use the "boys," hence they must be kept in reserve and cannot deliberately be put on the front line until the start of the 1.30 p.m. turn. Though the cadets had not seen combat, many of their adult officers and non-commissioned officers had previous combat experience, and the morale and excitement of the Cadet Corps was high; hence they are rated as Trained troops. Historically, at about 2 p.m. a large gap opened in the Confederate lines, and the VMI Cadets were the last viable reserves. Breckinridge was at first reluctant to commit them. Then Major Charles Sample said "they are of the best Virginia blood, they will stand." Breckinridge nodded, and with tears in his eyes ordered, "Put the boys in and may God forgive me for the order."

HISTORICAL OUTCOME

Breckinridge began his steady northward advance about 11 a.m. and would begin his main attack against Moor's Brigade a little before noon. Despite tough resistance, Moor's Brigade was gradually pushed back towards the rest of Sigel's army, which was trying to form a defensive line on the high ground of the Bushong Farm. About 1.30 p.m., the Confederates reformed to renew their attack on this new line, but massed Union defensive fire forced the Rebel center to give way and created a gap in their line. It was at that point that Breckenridge reluctantly committed the VMI cadets. At nearly the same time, Sigel launched a series of regimental counterattacks, which regained some ground but were eventually checked. Finally, almost in desperation, Stahel attempted a mounted charge with his cavalry, which was severely punished by the Confederate artillery. At this point, Breckinridge ordered a general advance and the Union line began to unravel; soon entire units were breaking towards the rear. As the retreat became a rout, five guns were eventually abandoned to the advancing Confederates, one of which was captured by the VMI cadets.

Breckinridge's victory was sweet, but soon soured because the day after the battle the general made a decision that negated much of the positive effect of his victory. The Kentuckian believed that the Army of the Shenandoah was beaten and demoralized and could make no major offensive moves in the valley for a long time to come. However, Breckinridge also realized that the strength of his army was insufficient to pursue the enemy and clear the valley of enemy troops. Therefore, he concluded that the war in the valley had resulted in stalemate, and that his veteran infantry could safely move to reinforce Lee's hard-pressed army at Spotsylvania and Cold Harbor. Lee agreed. Therefore, on the day following the battle, the grizzled victors of New Market – including the VMI cadets – marched to Staunton, where they jumped on flatcars and rode the Virginia Central Railroad to join Lee's forces outside of Richmond. Brigadier General John Imboden's cavalry brigade and the Valley District reserves were all that remained to garrison the valley. Almost as importantly, General Grant did not suffer a foolish general gladly and would unceremoniously sack Sigel immediately after the battle. Then on May 19, Grant raised Major General David "Black Dave" Hunter to command of the department, a man who had no interest in leisurely advances and mock battles.

ORDER OF BATTLE

WEAPON ABBREVIATIONS

RM: Rifle muskets, RC/P: Repeating carbines and pistols, MM/P: Mixed muskets and pistols, MM: Mixed muskets, SBLC/P: Sharps breech-loading carbines and pistols.

ARMY OF THE SHENANDOAH

MAJOR GENERAL FRANZ SIGEL (1 LB)
General Sigel was not present at the start of the battle. He arrives at the start of the Union 12.30 p.m. turn.
Infantry Division – Brigadier General Jeremiah Sullivan (1 LB)
   Sullivan does not arrive unit the Union 2 p.m. Active Turn (see reinforcements below)
Moor's "Ad Hoc" Brigade – Colonel Augustus Moor (1 LB)
   This was more of an *ad hoc* brigade than a formalized structure, as it fought at New Market with two regiments from Moor's own brigade and two from Colonel Thoburn's Brigade.
- 18th Connecticut Infantry – 599 men – 9 figures – RM – Trained
- 1st West Virginia Infantry – 360 men – 6 figures – RM – Veteran

- 34th Massachusetts Infantry – 500 men – 9 figures – RM – Veteran
- 123rd Ohio Infantry – 616 men – 10 figures – RM – Trained
- Snow's Battery (B/1st Maryland Light) – 3 sections – Mixed Guns – Veteran
- Von Kleiser's Battery (30th New York Battery) – three sections of Napoleons – Veteran

2nd Brigade (Minus) – Colonel Joseph Thoburn (1 LB)
- 54th Philadelphia Infantry – 566 men – 10 figures – RM – Veteran
- 1/12th West Virginia Infantry – 470 men – 8 figures – RM – Green
- 2/12th West Virginia Infantry – 459 men – 8 figures – RM – Green
- Carlin's Battery (D/1st West Virginia Light Artillery) – three sections of 3"Rifles – Veteran

Infantry Division Reinforcements
   Arrives in this order at the Union 2 p.m. active turn
- DuPont's Battery (B/5th US Light Artillery) – three sections of 3" Rifles – Elite
- Brigadier General Jeremiah Sullivan (1 LB)
- 28th Ohio Infantry- 574 men – 9 figures – RM – Trained
- 116th Ohio Infantry – 766 men – 12 figures – RM – Green

Cavalry Division – Brigadier General Julius Stahel (1 LB)
   All Union cavalry units start mounted. If they dismount they must stay dismounted for the entire scenario, unless they remount for the sole reason of retiring from the field and then must immediately retreat off the gameboard.
1st Cavalry Brigade (Minus) – Colonel William Tibbits (2 LB)
- 1st Maryland, Potomac Home Guard Cavalry – 360 men – 12 figures – BLC/P – Trained
- 1st New York Lincoln Cavalry – 270 men – 9 figures – RC/P – Trained
- 1st New York Veteran Cavalry – 270 men – 9 figures – RC/P – Veteran
- 14th Philadelphia Cavalry – 120 men – 4 figures – SBLC /P – Veteran
- 21st New York Cavalry – 120men – 4 figures – SBLC/P – Trained
- Ewing's Battery (G/1st West Virginia Light) – three sections – 3" Rifles – Veteran

2nd Cavalry Brigade – Colonel John Wynkoop (1 LB)
- 20th Philadelphia Cavalry – 120 men – 4 figures – SBLC/P – Veteran

- 22nd Philadelphia Cavalry – 120 men – 4 figures – RC/P – Veteran
- 15th New York Cavalry – 120 men – 4 figures – SBLC/P – Veteran

ARMY OF THE VALLEY DISTRICT
Major General John C. Breckenridge (2 LB)
Echols' Brigade – Colonel George S. Patton (1 LB)

Although Brigadier John Echols was this brigade's nominal commander, his worsening illness made Colonel Patton its *de facto* leader for most of the battle, and one week after the battle this arrangement was made official. Patton's performance at New Market would earn him a brigadier's commission, but he would be killed at the Battle of Winchester before it could be officially confirmed.

Although officially part of Echol's Brigade, the 26th VA would spend most of the battle fighting as part of Wharton's Brigade.

- 22nd Virginia Infantry – 540 men – 9 figures – RM – Elite (also known as the Kanawha Regiment)
- 23rd Virginia Infantry – 480 men – 8 figures – RM – Veteran
- 26th Virginia Infantry – 480 men – 8 figures – RM – Veteran

Wharton's Brigade – Brigadier General Gabriel Wharton (1 LB)

The 62nd VA was detached from the Valley Cavalry and fought as any other infantry. Its own 500 troopers were augmented by additional dismounted cavalry companies from the 18th Virginia, the 23th Virginia and the 1st Missouri Cavalry.

- 30th Virginia Infantry – 360 men – 6 figures – RM – Elite
- 51st Virginia Infantry – 630 men – 10 figures – RM – Veteran
- 62nd Virginia Infantry – 720 men – 12 figures – RM – Veteran

- VMI Cadet Battalion – 240 men – 4 figures – RM – Trained
- Jackson's Virginia Battery – 2 sections – Mixed Guns – Veteran

Cavalry Brigade – Brigadier General John Imboden (2 LB)

- 1/18th Virginia Cavalry – 240 men – 8 figures – SBLC/P – Veteran
- 2/18th Virginia Cavalry – 240 men – 8 figures – SBLC/P – Veteran
- 23rd Virginia Cavalry – 240 men – 8 figures – MM/P – Veteran
- McClanahan's Virginia Battery – two sections of mixed guns – Veteran (also known as the Staunton Horse Artillery)

Artillery Battalion – Major William McLaughlin (1 Arty LB)

Berkeley's section detached from McClanahan's Battery

- Chapman's Virginia Battery – three sections – mixed guns – Veteran
- Berkeley's Section – one section of 3" Rifles – Elite
- Captain Minge's VMI Section – one section of 3" Rifles – Veteran

Valley Reserves – Colonel William Harman (no LB)

Since they were almost raw recruits, Breckinridge did not commit them to battle. However, after a few weeks more of training, some of the same elements of the Valley Reserves would do well enough at the Battle of Piedmont. They enter at 1 p.m. and go into reserve in New Market. Beginning with the 1 p.m. turn, roll 1D6 at the start of each Confederate active turn for release; it takes 1 or 2 for their release. If released, they can be used freely.

- Augusta-Rockingham Reserves – 480 men – 8 figures – MM – Green

HUNTER TAKES COMMAND - PIEDMONT

Shenandoah Valley, Cedar Creek, Early Evening, May 21, 1864, by Dean West

THE WAR DEPARTMENT, LATE EVENING, MAY 18, 1864, WASHINGTON, DC

Secretary of War Henry Halleck had just informed Lieutenant General Ulysses S. Grant that contrary to the earlier *New York Times* report that General Sigel had "whipped the Rebels", it was Sigel's army that was in full retreat from New Market. He went on to tell Grant that

"Sigel will do nothing but run. He never did anything else." Grant became enraged, and when Halleck recommended that Sigel be replaced by Major General David Hunter, Grant responded, "By all means ... appoint General Hunter or anyone else to the command of West Virginia." The next day, May 19, the War Department made it official – Sigel would be gone.

When Major General David Hunter arrived at Sigel's headquarters to formally relieve him of command,

General Sullivan prepares to lead the attack against the Piedmont defenses. (Dean West)

General Sigel was not there. While waiting for Sigel to arrive, Colonel David Strother, Sigel's aide-de-camp, chatted with Hunter about the battle and said, "We can afford to lose such a battle as New Market, to get rid of such a mistake as Major General Sigel." Later that night, Sigel arrived and the command of the Army of the Shenandoah officially passed to Major General "Black David" Hunter. Serious war was about to come to the Valley.

General Hunter proved to be the right man, in the right place, at the right time. Hunter was a West Point graduate and among the most senior general officers in the United States Army. He had commanded a brigade at First Bull Run, but due to excessive zeal in recruiting former slaves as soldiers while commanding the Department of the South, he had been relegated to various desk jobs since September of 1862. However, he was well aware that success in the Valley would resurrect his stagnated career, and he seized this unexpected promotion with exceptional energy and fervent ambition.

Upon taking command, Hunter was surprised and excited to find that the Army of the Shenandoah remained battleworthy and that its soldiers were angrier at Sigel's inept generalship than demoralized by their defeat at New Market. Immediately Hunter went to work to repair deficiencies in the army's equipment and organization, and within a short time there were noticeable improvements. Then it got better. Within a few days, Hunter received the very welcome news that Breckinridge and his veteran units had left the Valley for Lee's army outside Richmond, leaving only Imboden's cavalry and the green recruits of the Valley Reserves to contest his planned advance. This was an opportunity that was not to be missed. On May 26, just 11 days following their defeat at New Market, the soldiers of the Army of the Shenandoah filed onto the Valley Pike and eagerly headed south toward Staunton. It was time to give Johnnie Reb some payback.

AN UNEXPECTED CRISIS

The ever-vigilant Brigadier General John Imboden was quick to advise General Lee that, contrary to Breckinridge's optimistic report, the Federals in the Valley were not about to accept a stalemate and were now moving south with renewed energy and spirit. This presented Lee with a conundrum. The Confederacy could not afford to lose the Valley, but Lee could not spare a single soldier from the Richmond front as he struggled to contain Grant's relentless drive south. In addition to the

major rail centers of Staunton and Lynchburg, the Shenandoah Valley remained a vital source of foodstuffs and other war materials supplying Robert E. Lee's army outside of Richmond; it had to be protected. The Valley lay exposed, and Imboden did not exaggerate the desperate nature of the situation when he wrote to Lee, "There is no place ... where I can successfully resist him ... though I will do my best."

A GRUMBLING CURMUDGEON STEPS UP

The only troops that Lee could tap were 200 miles away across the mountains of West Virginia and were under the command of the eccentric, cantankerous, and argumentative Brigadier General William E. "Grumble" Jones. However, Jones was a solid tactical leader and his men were tough and experienced fighters, both exactly what Lee needed right then in the Shenandoah Valley. On May 30, Lee ordered Jones and as many troops as he could bring to move immediately from East Tennessee and take command of the Valley District Army.

Fortunately, most of Jones' soldiers were currently deployed along the Virginia and Tennessee Railroad that ran directly from Tennessee into the Valley. Within a day, the ever-resourceful Jones gathered his superb little Trans-Allegheny army onto the creaky cars of that overused railroad and within four days, 2,400 infantry, 1,500 dismounted cavalry and a six-gun battery had been moved to the Valley, with Jones' mounted force catching up later. When added to Imboden's cavalry and the Valley Reserves, the Confederates now had over 5,500 men to block Hunter's 8,500. It was a close-run thing, but the Valley was again defended.

MOVES AND COUNTERMOVES

By June 3, the Hunter's Army had reached Harrisonburg. Their cavalry found the now-combined forces of Grumble Jones and John Imboden blocking their advance at Mount Crawford in a strong position behind the North River. On June 4, preferring a flanking maneuver to a bloody assault, Hunter sent a small diversionary cavalry force to demonstrate in front of the Mount Crawford position, while he led the bulk of the Army of the Shenandoah in a flanking march to Port Republic which he reached that night.

Despite a persistent rain, Imboden's scouts reported Hunter's flank march to "Grumble" who would respond

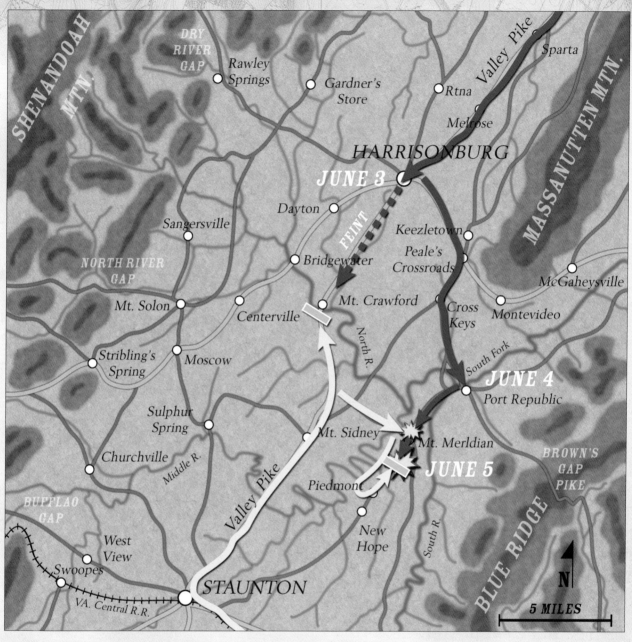

The Armies Converge on Piedmont, June 3 through June 5, 1864.

with some quick marching of his own. Imboden was ordered to take all the mounted cavalry and to intercept and delay Hunter's forces, while Jones took the rest of the force and prepared a new defensive position south of Mount Meridian.

Early on June 5, Imboden's mounted force attacked Stahel's cavalry outside Mount Meridian. At first, the graycoats had the advantage, but Stahel had the numbers and soon the Rebels were fleeing southward. Barely escaping with his skin, Imboden discovered that Jones was preparing a defensive line in front of the little town of Piedmont. Imboden, a native of the Valley, recommended a better position further south at Mowry's Hill. But cranky old "Grumble" had made his decision and ended the discussion with a sharp "I command here today sir … and I'm going to fight right here." And so the battle would be at Piedmont.

SCENARIO SPECIFIC RULES

SCENARIO LENGTH, INITIATIVE AND VICTORY CONDITIONS

The scenario begins with the 10 a.m. turn and continues until the end of the 2 p.m. turn, for a total of 9 turns. The Union has the initiative and will be active first. The Union command has 9 turns in which to capture Piedmont. If at the end of any one turn, the Union completely controls the Piedmont town area, they have won and the game has ended. For the Union to claim control of the Piedmont town area, they must have at least three non-routed units in the Piedmont town area and there must be no Confederate units within that area.

The Confederates win if they can prevent the Union from achieving their victory condition, or if they are able to successfully occupy any section of the East Staunton Road in the northeast square of the battlefield for any three consecutive turns. This second Confederate victory option reflects General Hunter's sensitivity to his line of communications leading back to Strasburg.

TERRAIN

TERRAIN DESCRIPTION

The terrain in the Piedmont area was typical of this part of the Shenandoah Valley. Most of the slopes were gentle, with occasional steep areas or impassable bluffs. Since the area was heavily farmed with freely grazing animals, all the woods are considered light woods. It is early June and the crops are low, so all the fields are treated as open ground, with no visibility blockage. The area designated as a "flood plain" is open ground. The Middle River is considered to be two inches of rough terrain and any unit crossing it ends its crossing in disorder. The smaller streams, such as "Polecat Draft," are considered to be one inch of broken terrain.

GOING UP SLOPES

If in any one movement action a unit goes up two elevation differences – such as going up from Level 1 to Level 3 – the movement is made at one category worse than if it was level ground. If, however, the unit only moved up one elevation level in any one movement action, the move is made as if it was level terrain. The terrain levels are indicated on the map.

THE HASTY WORKS

These were quickly constructed that morning by scavenging fence rails from most of the farms and fields in the area. Hence, there are two lines of hasty works and not many remaining fences. Units in the hasty works in the light woods on the higher Level 3 hill – the Confederates called this position the "The Rail Pen" – have the target cover benefits of both light woods (0/-1 DRM) and hasty works (-2 DRM for all fires) for a net target benefit of (-2 DRM) against artillery fire and a (-3 DRM) against all other fires. Given the overall strength of this position – it resisted multiple determined Union attacks and was not taken until the whole position was flanked – it gives its defender the heavy cover morale benefit of (-2 MMP). The other hasty works along the cross road are in the open, so they only have the normal hasty works target benefit of (-2 DRM from all fire) and give the defender the light cover morale benefit of (-1 MMP).

THE TOWN OF PIEDMONT

The town area itself was small, and its cover and morale benefit is equivalent to a farm area in terms of target DRM benefits (-1 DRM against artillery/-3 DRM against infantry fire) and light cover (-1 MMP) morale benefit. Units fighting from inside the town area have their FPs halved, unless they are on positioned exactly on the edge of the town area and are firing at a target outside the town area. Individual buildings have no specific effect.

DEAD GROUND

The "Dead Ground" is the area immediately behind the small Level 2 hill in front of the wheat field. This little hill is high enough to block visibility behind it. Confederate units in the hasty works that are on Level 3 terrain can see over this little hill, except into the indicated "Dead Ground" area of the map. Units crossing over this Level 2 hill are not seen by the units in the wheat field directly beyond or those in the hasty works until they get to the top of the little hill.

CRAWFORD'S RUN RAVINE

Most of the length of Crawford's Run is a shallow sunken ravine, which is treated as two inches of light woods for any movement across it, while units moving along the ravine make the entire move as if moving through light

HUNTER TAKES COMMAND - PIEDMONT

Brigade commanders set up with any unit of their brigade. Division commanders set up with of their formation. Army commanders set up anywhere on their side.

11:00 AM 4WV REG.
Arrives in road column.

12:30 PM W. JONES' BDE W. JONES' Bde. Arrives in road column.

Map by: Dean West & Todd Davis

---

woods. Units deployed in this ravine are visible, but receive a beneficial target -1 DRM against all fire and a -1 MMP modifier for all morale checks. Units attempting to charge across this ravine go into disorder upon leaving the ravine. The non-ravine sections of Crawford's Run and Pole Cat Draft are considered to be one inch of broken ground. Where the ravine ends, treat Crawford's Run as a small stream.

ROCKY BRUSH

The northwest slope of Sheep Hill was covered with a nasty rocky brush that is treated as light woods for infantry and dismounted cavalry moving down or along a slope, but heavy woods for infantry or dismounted cavalry going upslope. Mounted cavalry and artillery treat it as

rough terrain for all movements. Units can see into the rocky brush up to a distance of one inch for all scales, but units cannot see through it. Units in the rocky brush have a beneficial target -1 DRM against infantry or artillery fire, but have no target DRM benefits against artillery fire. There is no morale benefit for being in the rocky brush, as the troops did not like being there.

THE BLUFFS

The area marked as the bluff is just that – a very steep bluff impassable in all directions.

TERRAIN REPRESENTATION

Each terrain level beyond Level 1 represents a rise of about ½ inch for 10mm figures, ¾ inch for 15mm figures or one inch for 25mm figures. Level 1 is the tabletop surface and has no elevation. However, the amount of rise per level can certainly be adjusted per personal preference, as smaller elevation differences can often look more realistic depending on the terrain being modeled.

UNION SET-UP
The Army of the Shenandoah begins the game deployed as shown in the northeast corner of the game board. All units must set up exactly where indicated on the map, except that one battery may be redeployed anywhere along the Union line but no closer to an enemy unit than is any other friendly formed infantry, cavalry or artillery unit. The cavalry brigades on the game board are deployed as shown on the map, but unlike the infantry, regimental designation of individual units within the brigade designations is not shown. Peale's Sharpshooters must start in skirmish order in the woods. If not specified, leaders can come in with any unit in their command.

CONFEDERATE SET-UP
Most of the Army of the Valley District begins the game deployed exactly as indicated on the battle map, except that one battery may be redeployed anywhere along the Confederate line, but not within 15 inches of a formed Union unit or battery. The map symbols for the infantry regiments of Browne's and B. Jones' brigades include unit designations in order to show their actual historical place in the battle line. Most cavalry map symbols are not unit specific, so any unit of the appropriate brigade may be placed where these symbols appear. If not specified, leaders can start or come with any unit of their command.

HISTORICAL OUTCOME
Following the morning defeat of Imboden's cavalry at Mount Meridian, General Hunter and the Army of the Shenandoah arrived at Confederate position just north of Piedmont. After clearing the northwest hill, Colonel David Strother rode up and surveyed the Confederate position and realized that this would be hard work. He would describe it as: "The enemy's position was strong and well chosen. It was on a conclave of wooded hills commanding an open valley between and open, gentle slopes in front. On our right in advance of the village of Piedmont was a line of log and rail defenses very advantageously located in the edge of a forest."

And hard work it was. Moor's Brigade would assault the "rail pen" no less than three times, but each time the veteran brigades of Jones and Browne threw him back with heavy losses. As the third attack recoiled in confusion, the defending Confederates counterattacked, and only a gallant stand by a battalion of repeater-armed New York cavalry troopers, and a section of guns broke the Rebel rush and drove them back into their works. Initially seeing yet another Union repulse, Grumble Jones decided to expand on Moor's discomfiture and ordered most of Vaughn's Brigade to move against the disordered attackers. This potential counterstroke had unexpected consequences. The movement weakened a thin Confederate center, which already had a substantial gap and had seen its artillery support gradually driven off by superior massed Federal artillery.

After a morning of frustrated assaults, this was the opportunity that "Black David" was hoping for. He ordered Thoburn's Brigade to turn into the thinly-held Confederate center and press the Rebel flank, while Moor renewed his frontal the attack against the "rail pen." With pressure on both front and flank, the Confederate defense finally folded and soon the graybacks were streaming to the rear. Old "Grumble" threw in the Valley Reserves, but they were unable to contain the growing disaster. Finally, the feisty curmudgeon rallied a group of veterans, leading them in a desperate counter-charge against the advancing bluecoats, and was promptly shot in the head. That was the last straw – the retreat became a rout. The Union committed Stahel's cavalry and the roundup of the fugitives began. While the Union lost 875 killed and wounded, the Confederate lost almost 1,400, with about 1,000 of those being captured. Despite a spirited rear-guard defense at New Hope on June 6, David Hunter became the first Union commander to lead a victorious army deep into the Shenandoah Valley, capturing Staunton, burning VMI, and threatening the vital rail center of Lynchburg. This triggered a new crisis for Robert E. Lee, which would require the dispatching of the bulk of Jubal Early's Corps to the Shenandoah Valley.

ORDER OF BATTLE

WEAPON ABBREVIATIONS

RM: Rifle muskets, **RC/P:** Repeating carbines and pistols, **MM/P:** Mixed muskets and pistols, **MM:** Mixed muskets, **SBLC/P:** Sharps breech-loading carbines and pistols.

ARMY OF THE SHENANDOAH

MAJOR GENERAL DAVID "BLACK DAVID" HUNTER (1 LB)

Infantry Division – Brigadier General Jeremiah Sullivan (1 LB)

First Brigade – Colonel Augustus Moor (1 LB)

By 1864 the Union was converting its well-trained garrison artillery units to infantry regiments, hence the 5th NY is deployed as an infantry regiment.

The 116th OH was serving as the wagon train guards and enters on the 11.30 p.m. turn on the north edge of East Staunton Road.

- 18th Connecticut Infantry – 540 men – 9 figures – RM – Veteran
- 5th New York Heavy Artillery (Inf Rgt) – 600 men – 10 figures – RM – Trained
- 28th Ohio Infantry – 600 men – 10 figures – RM – Elite
- 123rd Ohio Infantry – 600 men – 10 figures – RM – Veteran
- 116th Ohio Infantry – 480 men – 8 figures – RM – Veteran
- Peale's Battalion of Sharpshooters – 240 men – 4 figures – RM – Veteran

Second Brigade – Colonel Joseph Thoburn (1 LB)
- 2nd Maryland Eastern Shore Infantry – 480 men – 8 figures – RM – Veteran
- 34th Massachusetts Infantry – 540 men – 9 figures – RM – Elite
- 54th Philadelphia Infantry – 480 men – 8 figures – RM – Veteran
- 1st West Virginia Infantry – 600 men – 10 figures – RM – Veteran
- 12th West Virginia Infantry – 600 men – 10 figures – RM – Veteran
- 4th West Virginia Infantry – 480 men – 8 figures – RM – Trained

Artillery Battalion – Captain Henry Algeron du Pont (1 Artillery LB)
- Snow's Battery (B/Massachusetts Light Artillery) – 3 sections of 3" rifles – Veteran
- Von Klieiser's Battery (New York Light Artillery) – 3 sections of Napoleons – Veteran

- Holman's Battery (B/5th US Lt Artillery) – 3 sections of 3" Rifles – Elite
- Carlin's Battery (D/1st West Virginia Lt. Artillery) – 3 sections of 3" rifles – Veteran

Cavalry Division – Brigadier General Julius Stahel (1 LB)

Stahel's cavalry division has been heavily engaged against Imboden's cavalry for most of the morning, and consequently none of these cavalry units receive opening volley benefits. By this time, with the exception of Wynkoop's Brigade, the horses are blown and hence the units must fight dismounted.

First Brigade (minus) – Colonel Andrew McReynolds (All dismounted) (0 LB)

All of McReynold's brigade was ordered to dismount and fight on foot to support the infantry. Each unit should only use dismounted stands, recommended modeling is three stands per unit with 3 or 4 figures per stand.

- 1st Maryland Home Guard Cavalry – 360 men – 12 dismounted figures – BLC/P – Trained
- 1st New York Lincoln Cavalry – 270 men – 9 dismounted figures – RC/P – Veteran
- 1st New York Veteran Cavalry – 270 men – 9 dismounted figures – RC/P – Elite

Detachment From First Brigade – Colonel William Tibbits (All dismounted) (2 LB)

Recommend three stands of three figures each.
- 21st New York Cavalry – 270 men – 9 dismounted figures – BLC/P – Veteran
- 14th Philadelphia Cavalry – 270 men – 9 dismounted figures – BLC/P – Veteran

Second Brigade – Colonel John Wynkoop (1 LB)

Wynkoop's Brigade has not been as heavily engaged as McReynold's and Tibbitt's so its horses are somewhat fresher. Hence the troops can start mounted or dismounted. If they dismount, they may only remount to retire from the battlefield. Otherwise, once dismounted they must stay dismounted.
- 20th Philadelphia Cavalry – 480 men – 12 mounted/ dismounted figures – BLC/P – Veteran
- Ringgold Cavalry Battalion – 240 men – 8 mounted/ dismounted figures – BLC /P – Elite

THE ARMY OF THE VALLEY DISTRICT

BRIGADIER GENERAL WILLIAM "GRUMBLE" JONES (2 LB)
First Infantry Brigade – Colonel Buering Jones (1 LB)

Though they had minimal training, the Niter & Mining Battalion would fight like veterans.

- 36th Virginia Infantry – 540 men – 9 figures – RM – Veteran
- 60th Virginia Infantry – 600 men – 9 figures – RM – Veteran
- 45th Virginia Infantry – 300 men – 6 figures – RM – Veteran
- Bryan's Virginia Battery (Lewisburg Artillery) – 3 sections of mixed guns – Elite
- The Niter & Mining Battalion – 240 men – 4 figures – RM – Veteran

Second Infantry Brigade – Colonel William E. Browne (1 LB)

Although they were originally formed as cavalry, Brewer's Battalion fought as exactly as infantry, so they use the 60 men per figure ratio as infantry and move and fight using the Infantry Movement and Fire Tables.

- Additional Officer Figure: Major Brewer (1 LB)
- 45th Virginia Infantry – 617 men – 9 figures – RM – Veteran
- Thomas' North Carolina Legion – 440 men – 8 figures – RM – Veteran
- Brewer's Dismounted Cavalry Battalion – 540 men – 9 figures – RM – Elite

Valley Reserves – Colonel Kenton Harper (1 LB)

Marquis' Battery had at least one 20-Pounder Parrott and at least one 24-pounder howitzer, hence they have a firepower of 6 FP with a normal range of 16.

- Augusta Reserve Infantry – 720 men – 12 figures – MM – Trained
- Marquis' Battery – (The Augusta Reserve Artillery) – 2 sections of Mixed Heavy Guns (6 FP – NR 16) – Veteran

Cavalry Brigade – Brigadier General John Imboden (1 LB)

Imboden's Brigade had also absorbed two companies of the Augusta County Mounted Reserves.

The 18th and 23rd VA's horses were blown after the morning battle with Stahel's cavalry and needed to rest. Hence Imboden's Brigade must fight most of the battle as dismounted cavalry, using the Cavalry Movement and Fire Tables. However, at the 12.30 p.m. turn they can remount if desired, but must continue the remainder of the fight as mounted cavalry.

Davis' Cavalry Battalion included at least two companies of the Rockingham Country Reserves, whose horses were fresher; hence they can fight either mounted or dismounted. However, once they dismount they can only remount to retire from the battlefield.

- 18th Virginia Cavalry* – 360 men – 12 Dismounted Cavalry Figures – SBLC/P – Veteran
- 23rd Virginia Cavalry*- 270 men – 9 Dismounted Cavalry Figures – SBLC/P – Veteran
- Davis' Maryland Cavalry – 270 men – 9 Figures – MM – Veteran
- McClanahan's Virginia Battery (Lewisburg Artillery) – 3 sections of mixed guns – Veteran

Dismounted "Cavalry" Brigade – Brigadier General John C. Vaughn (1 LB)

Although they were originally formed as cavalry, this brigade fought exactly as infantry, so they use the 60 men per infantry figure ratio as infantry and move and fight using the Infantry Movement and Fire Tables.

Vaughan's Brigade also included fragments from the 16th Georgia and 16th Tennessee Cavalry along with men from the 43rd, 59th, 60th, 61st, and 62nd Tennessee Mounted Infantry.

- 39th & 3rd Tennessee, Mounted Infantry – 360 men – 6 Infantry Figures – RM – Veteran
- 1st & 12th Tennessee, Mounted Infantry – 480 men – 8 Infantry Figures – RM – Veteran
- 3rd & 53rd Tennessee, Mounted Infantry – 360 men – 6 Infantry Figures – MM – Veteran

Confederate Reinforcements

Arrive dismounted on the south edge of East Staunton Road on the 12.30 p.m. turn.

Brigadier General William E. Jones' "Cavalry" Brigade, Lieutenant Colonel Smith (1 LB) commanding

Although they were originally formed as cavalry, they fought as exactly as infantry, so they use the 60 men per infantry figure ratio and move and fight using the Infantry Movement and Fire Tables.

- 27th & 34th Virginia, Mounted Infantry – 360 men – 6 Infantry figures – RM – Elite
- 64th Virginia, Mounted Infantry – 440 men – 8 Infantry figures – RM – Veteran
- 8th & 21st Virginia Mounted Infantry – 360 men – 6 Infantry figures – MM – Veteran

BLACK COURAGE - NEW MARKET HEIGHTS

Pre-dawn, September 29, 1864, just south of New Market Heights

General Butler's plan had been daring. Just as darkness fell on the Federal lines at Bermuda Hundred, the bulk of the two corps of the Army of the James would withdraw behind a thin line of garrison troops and make a night march to the two pontoon bridges over the James River. Then, while it was still dark, the bulk of those corps would cross those bridges and deploy for a surprise attack at two points against the outer defenses of Richmond – all before sunup. To minimize traffic congestion and the noise of two corps on the move, almost all the artillery and cavalry of the Army of the James had been left in reserve on the south side of the Deep Bottom crossing. This would be a lighting infantry strike to open up the back door to Richmond. Despite the logistic challenges of a night march across a major river, the units were in place.

As General Butler rode among the black soldiers of Paine's Division forming up in the foggy woods fronting Four Mile Creek, he must have been a comical sight. No officer looked less like a military commander than overstuffed, stump-legged, pop-eyed Ben "The Beast" Butler, who almost enjoyed the contempt his southern opponents had for him. However, no general in the entire Union Army was a stronger supporter of the black soldiers that made up the United States Colored Troops than was he. And today he was determined to prove that they were much more than uniformed ditch diggers. He had been appalled at how they were misused at the Crater and how their white commanders had failed to lead them. That would not happen today, as he had planned this attack with 16 pages of detailed instructions. The task, however, was daunting, as the entrenched position facing his well-trained but not fully tested black regiments had twice rebuffed the great General Hancock and his highly regarded II Corps. Finally, as the first hint of dawn attempted to pierce the morning fog and the brigades began to move out, General Butler gave his black soldiers a final bit of encouragement as he told them to "Remember Fort Pillow!"

SCENARIO SPECIFIC RULES

SCENARIO LENGTH, INITIATIVE AND VICTORY CONDITIONS

The scenario starts with the 5 a.m. turn and goes until the end of the 8 a.m. turn, for a total of seven turns of battle. The Union has the initiative and is active first for the entire scenario. For the Union to win, they must capture and hold any two of the Confederate high ground artillery position behind the front lines by the end of the 8 a.m. turn: the one artillery position directly on the front lines does not count towards the Union victory conditions. The Confederates win if they can prevent that.

CONFEDERATE SETUP

The Confederates can set up using the picket system of numbered hidden units. For each real unit, the Confederates get one dummy picket. The Confederate player should record which picket number corresponds to which real unit. Both real and dummy units can be placed anywhere in or north of the Confederate heavy works. Both real and dummy pickets can move up to three inches per action or – if it is a real unit – use an action or reaction to fire. Once a real unit fires, it must be placed on the game table. Any time a Union unit gets within three inches of a picket, it is spotted and if it is a real unit, it must be placed on the table. If it is a dummy picket, it is removed.

CONFEDERATE MORALE DEGRADATION

Historically, once the works were breeched, the Confederates began heading for the rear. To reflect that, for every one of the high ground artillery positions the Union occupies, all Confederate units suffer an immediate +2 MMP morale penalty as long as that position is Union-occupied. If the Confederates retake that position, then the +2 MMP morale penalty immediately disappears.

UNION SETUP

The Union sets up each brigade in their designated brigade area in any formation they choose. On the 5 a.m. turn, the Union is limited to advancing one regiment per brigade forward as skirmishers. However, the brigades of Terry's Division – which had been assigned a supporting role – must keep all their regiments in their brigade area until they are released. The Union player rolls a 1D6 for the brigades in Terry's Division – Abbot's, Pond's and Plaisted's brigades – at the start of each of his active turns to see if these brigades are released from their reserve position. It takes a 1 or 2 them to be released. Likewise, the Corps reserve brigade of William Birney can only be released on a 1D6 roll of 1 rolled at the start of each Union active turn. Historically, W. Birney saw no action.

EXPANDED SCENARIO

The expanded scenario gives the Union the use of the entire 2nd Division of the X Corps, which arrives at 5.30 a.m. Historically, this division remained in reserve along the Grover House Road throughout the battle. The Confederates get all the artillery batteries of Hardaway's Virginia Artillery Battalion along with the automatic arrival of Benning's Brigade on the 6 a.m. turn.

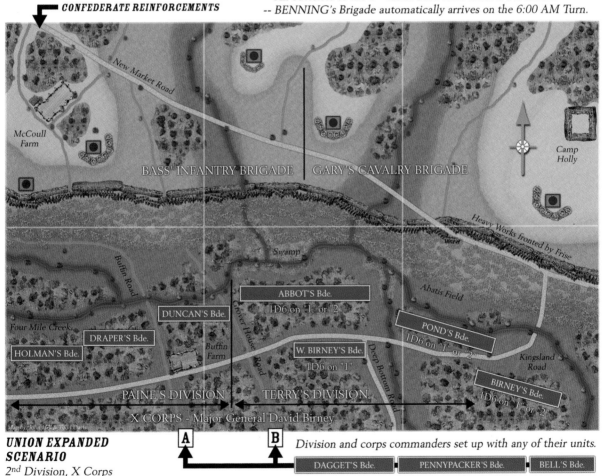

NEW MARKET HEIGHTS - SEPTEMBER 29, 1864

Brigade commanders set up with any unit of their brigades.

CONFEDERATE EXPANDED SCENARIO
-- CITY OF RICHMOND Bns. <u>start</u> anywhere in the heavy works.
-- All batteries of the 1st VA LIGHT ARTY. Bn. are available.
-- BENNING's Brigade automatically arrives on the 6:00 AM Turn.

CONFEDERATE REINFORCEMENTS

New Market Road

McCoull Farm

Camp Holly

BASS' INFANTRY BRIGADE   GARY'S CAVALRY BRIGADE

Heavy Works fronted by Frise

Swamp

Abatis Field

ABBOT'S Bde.
1D6 on "1" or "2"

POND'S Bde.
1D6 on "1" or "2"

DUNCAN'S Bde.

Buffin Road

Grover House Road

W. BIRNEY'S Bde.
1D6 on "1"

Deep Bottom Road

Kingsland Road

Four Mile Creek

DRAPER'S Bde.

Buffin Farm

BIRNEY'S Bde.
1D6 on "1" or "2"

HOLMAN'S Bde.

PAINE'S DIVISION   TERRY'S DIVISION

X CORPS - Major General David Birney

Map by John Hill & Rick Barts

A   **B**   Division and corps commanders set up with any of their units.

UNION EXPANDED SCENARIO
2nd Division, X Corps

DAGGET'S Bde.   PENNYPACKER'S Bde.   BELL'S Bde.

Brig. Gen'l. G. R. S. Foster: Enters in <u>one</u> road column as shown on Road Entrance "A" <u>or</u> "B" on the Union 5:30 AM urn.

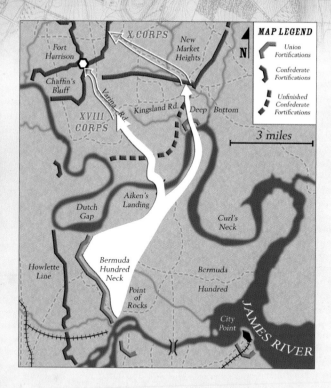

MAP LEGEND

Union
Fortifications

Confederate
Fortifications

Unfinished
Confederate
Fortifications

3 miles

The Expanded Scenario is also extended to the 9 a.m. turn for a scenario length of nine turns of battle. The Expanded Scenario also increases the Union victory conditions to any three of the Confederate high ground artillery positions.

TERRAIN DESCRIPTION

The area is classic tidewater low country. The streams and creeks are muddy, meandering and often spread out creating shallow swamps and marshes. The creeks in the scenario should be treated as one inch of heavy woods for movement and the swamps are treated as heavy woods in their entirety, but without any of the cover benefits of heavy woods. The slopes are gentle and there is no movement penalty for going up or down them. The dark gray roads are named and all other light gray roads are considered to be trails. A unit on a higher elevation can see over one on a lower elevation, but cannot fire over it unless it is two elevations higher. The woods are broken by two farms and have been thinned by grazing animals, so all woods are considered to be light woods.

THE HEAVY WORKS

Units firing from behind heavy works are not penalized for being in disorder, extended line or skirmish order, but

rather have a consistent heavy works firing benefit of +2 DRM. All infantry and artillery units in the heavy works receive a -4 DRM target benefit against all fires coming across the works regardless of the formation they are in. Units directly in the heavy works receive a -4 MMP benefit to all morale checks and affect dice-down resolutions unless the fire and/or charge is coming from behind the works, in which case there is no morale or target benefits.

Assume that the Confederate artillery revetments each hold only one battery and are positioned so that a battery in any of them on ground higher than the heavy works can do non-canister firing over any Confederate unit that is directly in those works, provided the target unit is over one away from any friendly unit. If the artillery is pulled out of the works, it can only fire over friendly units if it is two levels higher than the unit. Confederate artillery in the works has an arc of fire of 45 degrees without pivoting. It takes a full action for that artillery to pivot or to be pulled out of its revetments and re-limbered as field artillery.

THE ABATIS FIELD

Rather than a single abatis of a line of tightly packed felled trees, New Market Heights was protected by an abatis field that was deeper but less dense than a traditional linear abatis. Units moving through the abatis field do so at the heavy woods movement rate, and all charges into or out of the abatis field are done in disorder, with only a 1D6 charge bonus. The abatis field gives no protection from fire. The abatis field is two inches deep for 10mm, three inches deep for 15mm, and four inches deep for 25mm games. There is clear ground of two inches for all figure scales between the edge of the abatis field and the fraise (see below).

THE OBSTACLES

It is unclear as to whether the front line heavy works were protected by a fraise or chevaux-de-frise. However, for this scenario, use either and treat either simply as an inch of rough terrain, with all charges across them being done in disorder and the total charge distance, if successful, being limited to occupying the works beyond.

UNCAPPED MUSKETS

A few of the more experienced officers, having seen attacks against entrenchments falter because the soldiers would stop and attempt to fire back at soldiers protected by heavy works, ordered their troops to charge with unloaded or uncapped muskets. This forced the attacker to keep going and take the position with the bayonet. To do this requires two declared actions – "this unit(s) will be charging with empty muskets" – with the last action being a charge. Units so doing cannot fire this active turn, but get a -1 MMP benefit throughout their active turn. For the following reaction, assume loaded muskets.

THE FOG

The attack was started in a heavy morning fog that gradually lifted as the sun came up. Hence, maximum visibility for the 5 p.m. and 5.30 a.m. turns is 6"/12"/18" for 10mm/15mm/25mm figures respectively. For the 6 and 6.30 a.m. turns it is 12"/18"/24" respectively and unlimited visibility starting with the 7 a.m. turn.

HISTORICAL OUTCOME

Conceptually, Butler's concept of a dual simultaneous attack both against New Market Heights and up the Varina Road towards Fort Harrison was validated, as it presented the Confederates with two crises in an area where they would have enough resources only to deal with one. At New Market Heights, the Confederates easily rebuffed the initial attack, since it was done piecemeal without any mutual support. After regrouping, however, the Federals were able to break into the works at three different points, which ended the issue and precipitated a full Confederate retreat. Despite heavy losses, the Texas line was first breached by Holman's Brigade with the 22nd USCT in the lead, quickly followed by Draper's Brigade with the 5th USCT in the lead. Gary's cavalry line was outflanked and rolled up by the 3rd New Hampshire and the 24th Massachusetts of Terry's Division.

The Confederates responded by sending Benning's Brigade under Colonel DuBose first to New Market Heights and then recalled it to help defend Fort Harrison. The recall of DuBose was quickly followed by a general recall from New Market Heights, as a possible Union penetration beyond Fort Harrison was deemed more serious than the loss of New Market Height. It appears that the final breach of the Confederate line happened just about then. Whether the Confederates simply evacuated or were driven continues to be debated. But one fact remains: the cost for taking New Market Heights for the Paine's USCT Division had been high. About 800 of its 1,300 men were killed, wounded or missing, and of the 16 Congressional Medals of Honor given to black soldiers in the Civil War 14 of them were earned on New Market Heights. The following actual participants tell the story of their courage.

The Union Perspective: "It was a deadly hailstorm of bullets sweeping men down as a hailstorm sweeps leaves from a tree." – Sergeant Major Christian Fleetwood, 4th USCT, awarded Congressional Medal of Honor

The Confederate Perspective: "No troops up to that time had fought us with more bravery than did those Negro soldiers." – J. D. Pickens, Texas Brigade

The Commander's Perspective: "The capacity of the negro race for soldiers had then and there been fully settled forever." – Major General Benjamin F. Butler

Ben Butler's two-pronged offensive did take New Market Heights and Fort Harrison, which collapsed the exterior ring of Richmond's southeast defenses, and in that regard the offensive was an operational success. It did not, however, as General Butler had hoped, make a strategic breakthrough that would have opened the back door to Richmond. Lee was quick enough to respond to the threat and reserves were promptly shuttled up from Petersburg. However, it did force Lee to make some costly counterattacks and added another tightening of the noose that Grant was slowly wrapping around the Richmond and Petersburg defenses.

ORDER OF BATTLE

WEAPON ABBREVIATIONS

RM: Rifle muskets, **RC/P:** Repeating carbines and pistols, **MM/P:** Mixed muskets and pistols, **MM:** Mixed muskets, **SBLC/P:** Sharps breech-loading carbines and pistols, **RM/P:** Rifle muskets and pistols.

ARMY OF THE JAMES

MAJOR GENERAL BENJAMIN F. BUTLER (1 LB)

(2 LB) morale benefit when rallying USCT regiments. However, Butler cannot advance beyond Four Mile Creek.

X CORPS - MAJOR GENERAL DAVID B. BIRNEY (1LB)

The X Corps had may have had as many as 16,000 men when it first pulled out of the Bermuda Hundred lines, but straggling on the night march to New Market Heights probably reduced it to slightly less than 12,000 men.
1st Brigade/Third Division – Brigadier General William Birney (1 LB)

Corps Reserve – brother of the Corps Commander. This brigade was kept safely in reserve and saw no action. Roll 1D6 each turn for release only after all three brigades of Terry's Division have been released. It takes a 1 for the brigade to be released.

- 29th Connecticut – 360 men – 6 figures – RM – Veteran
- 7th United States Colored Troops – 360 men – 6 figures – RM – Veteran
- 8th United States Colored Troops – 360 men – 6 figures – RM – Veteran
- 9th United States Colored Troops – 360 men – 6 figures – RM – Veteran
- 45th United States Colored Troops – 480 men – 8 figures – RM – Trained

First Division – Brigadier Alfred H. Terry (1 LB)

Historically, the division was initially held back as support and was not fully committed to the attack until about 7 a.m. After being committed, the 24th Massachusetts and the 3rd New Hampshire eventually outflanked Gary's Cavalry Brigade.

1st Brigade – Colonel Francis Pond (1 LB)

Beginning with the 5 a.m. turn, roll 1D6 each turn for brigade release. It takes a 1 or 2 for release.

- 39th Illinois – 240 men – 4 figures – RM – Elite
- 62nd Ohio – 360 men – 6 figures – RM – Veteran
- 67th Ohio – 360 men – 6 figures – RM – Veteran
- 85th Philadelphia – 360 men – 6 figures – RM – Veteran

2nd Brigade – Colonel Joseph Abbot (1 LB)

Beginning with the 5 a.m. turn, roll 1D6 each turn for brigade release. It takes a 1 or 2 for release.

- 3rd New Hampshire – 240 men – 4 figures – RM – Elite
- 6th Connecticut – 360 men – 6 figures – RM – Veteran
- 7th Connecticut – 360 men – 6 figures – RM – Veteran
- 7th New Hampshire – 360 men – 6 figures – RM – Veteran
- 16th New York Heavy Artillery – 480 men – 8 figures – RM – Trained

3rd Brigade – Colonel Harris Plaisted (1 LB)

Beginning with the 5 a.m. turn, roll 1D6 each turn for brigade release. It takes a 1 or 2 for release.

- 10th Connecticut – 240 men – 4 figures – RM – Elite
- 11th Maine – 360 men – 6 figures – RM – Veteran
- 24th Massachusetts – 360 men – 6 figures – RM – Veteran
- 100th New York – 360 men – 6 figures – RM – Veteran
- 1st Maryland Cavalry – Used as divisional provost guard (not available)

Second Division – Brigadier Robert S. Foster (1 LB)

Historically, Foster's division was kept in reserve along the Grover House Road and was never committed to this attack.

1st Brigade – Colonel Rufus Daggett (1 LB)

- 3rd New York – 240 men – 4 figures – RM – Elite
- 112th New York – 360 men – 6 figures – RM – Veteran
- 117th New York – 360 men – 6 figures – RM – Veteran
- 142nd New York – 360 men – 6 figures – RM – Trained

2nd Brigade – Colonel Galusha Pennypacker (1 LB)

- 47th New York – 360 men – 6 figures – RM – Veteran
- 48th New York – 360 men – 6 figures – RM – Veteran
- 76th Philadelphia – 360 men – 6 figures – RM – Veteran
- 97th Philadelphia – 360 men – 6 figures – RM – Veteran
- 203rd Philadelphia – 480 men – 8 figures – RM – Trained

3rd Brigade – Colonel Louis Bell (1 LB)

- 13th Indiana – 240 men – 4 figures – RM – Elite
- 4th New Hampshire – 240 men – 4 figures – RM – Elite
- 9th Maine – 360 men – 6 figures – RM – Veteran
- 115th New York – 360 men – 6 figures – RM – Veteran
- 169th New York – 480 men – 8 figures – RM – Trained

Third Division/XVIII Corps – Brigadier General Charles J. Paine (1 LB)

Paine's division of about 3,800 men was attached to X Corps for the attack on New Market Heights. Though the black brigades had good officers, their division commander, Brigadier General Charles Paine, was unskilled and initially committed the brigades piecemeal. On the first assault, Duncan's Brigade was mauled by the Texans, but Colonel Draper then organized a second assault with his and Holman's brigades, which eventually broke the Texan's position.

1st Brigade – Colonel John H. Holman (1 LB)

- 1st United States Colored Troops – 360 men – 6 figures – RM – Veteran
- 22nd United States Colored Troops – 480 men – 8 figures – RM – Veteran
- 37th United States Colored Troops – 480 men – 8 figures – RM – Trained

2nd Brigade – Colonel Alonzo G. Draper (1 LB)

The 36th USCT was originally recruited in North Carolina in August 1863 as the 2nd North Carolina Colored Volunteers.

- 5th United States Colored Troops – 360 men – 6 figures – RM – Veteran
- 36th United States Colored Troops – 480 men – 8 figures – RM – Veteran

- 38th United States Colored Troops – 480 men – 8 figures – RM – Trained

3rd Brigade – Colonel Samuel A. Duncan (1 LB)
- 4th United States Colored Troops – 360 men – 6 figures – RM – Veteran
- 6th United States Colored Troops – 360 men – 6 figures – RM – Veteran
- 10th United States Colored Troops – 480 men – 8 figures – RM – Trained

Independent – 2nd USCT Cavalry – Not involved, strength unknown.

THE CONFEDERATE FORCES

Due to the small number of Confederate units and the large frontages to be held, it is recommended that the six-figure Confederate units be modeled as three-stand units with two figures per stand. Estimates for the total number of Confederate defenders vary from as low as 1,800 to as many as 3,000 men.

I CORPS, FIELD'S DIVISION, MAJOR GENERAL CHARLES FIELD (1 LB) (NOT PRESENT)
Area Commander: Brigadier General John Gregg (1 LB)
    Starts at Camp Holly.
Gregg's Texas Brigade – Lieutenant Colonel Frederick Bass (1 LB)
    To cover the available frontage, the 4th Texas and 5th Texas should probably be modeled with 3 stands of 2 figures each.
- 1st Texas – 240 men – 4 figures – RM – Elite
- 3rd Arkansas – 240 men – 4 figures – RM – Elite
- 4th Texas – 360 men – 6 figures – RM – Elite
- 5th Texas – 360 men – 6 figures – RM – Elite

Benning's Brigade – Colonel Dudley M. DuBose (1 LB)
Historically, they were sent as reinforcements to New Market Heights. But very soon after they got there, they were recalled and were countermarched to reinforce Fort Harrison, which was also under pressure from the Union XVIII Corps advancing up Varina Road. Unfortunately, by the time they arrived there, the fort had fallen and the battle was over. So for most of the morning, they spent most of their time moving back and forth and little time fighting. Beginning with the 6 a.m. turn, at the start of each Confederate active turn roll 1D6 for arrival; it takes a 1 or 2 for them to arrive on the north edge exit of the New Market Road. In the Expanded Scenario, they automatically arrive at 6 a.m.
- 2nd Georgia – 240 men – 4 figures – RM – Elite
- 17th Georgia – 240 men – 4 figures – RM – Veteran
- 15th Georgia – 360 men – 6 figures – RM – Veteran
- 20th Georgia – 360 men – 6 figures – RM – Veteran

1st Virginia Light Artillery Battalion – Lieutenant Colonel Richard A. Hardaway (1 LB) (not present)
The following batteries can set up in any of the artillery revetments, but only one battery per revetment. The 3rd Richmond Howitzers and Rockbridge Artillery are automatically available, but the Powhatan and Salem Virginia Artillery must each roll 1D6 at the start – they are available if they roll a 1 or 2. In the expanded scenario, all four batteries are available.
- 3rd Richmond Howitzers – two sections, 3" ordnance rifles – Veteran
- Rockbridge Artillery – two sections, 20 pdr Parrott rifles – Elite
- Powhatan Artillery – two sections 3" ordnance rifles – Veteran
- Salem Virginia Artillery – two sections, mixed guns – Veteran

Department of Richmond – Lieutenant General Richard S. Ewell (1 LB) (not present)
Gary's Cavalry Brigade – Brigadier General Martin W. Gary (1 LB)
Gary's brigade fights the entire scenario dismounted as their horses had been sent to the rear. The 24th Virginia Cavalry was formed in March 1864 from depleted companies of the 42nd Virginia Cavalry and Dearing's Cavalry Squadron.
- Hampton's Legion – 180 men – 6 figures – RM/P – Elite
- 7th South Carolina Cavalry – 180 men – 6 figures – RM/P – Veteran
- 24th Virginia Cavalry – 180 men – 6 figures – RM/P – Veteran

City of Richmond Battalions
These battalions arrive at 6 a.m. on the north exit of the New Market Road. In the Expanded Scenario, they start in the works.
- Elliot's 25th Virginia Reserve Battalion – 240 men – 4 figures – MM – Trained
- Guy's 2nd Virginia Reserve Battalion – 240 men – 4 figures – MM – Trained

CHARGING HEAVY WORKS

SIMPLIFYING IMPACT RESOLUTION

Whenever the two opposing units have equal situational MMP modifying factors – good or bad – do not include them in the final impact resolution calculation, as follows: since both opposing impact units are within two inches of the enemy, neither one suffers the +1 MMP detriment in charge impact resolution. Since both opposing impact units have a 1 LB leader with the lead impact unit, neither side gets the leader benefit for impact resolution. However, if one side had a 2 LB leader and the other side had a 1 LB leader, then just factor in the beneficial difference of 1 to the side that had the leader advantage

RESOLVING CHARGE IMPACT RESOLUTION

The highest Final Impact Value (FIV) wins. For each unit the FIV is calculated as follows: a unit's FIV equals 2D6

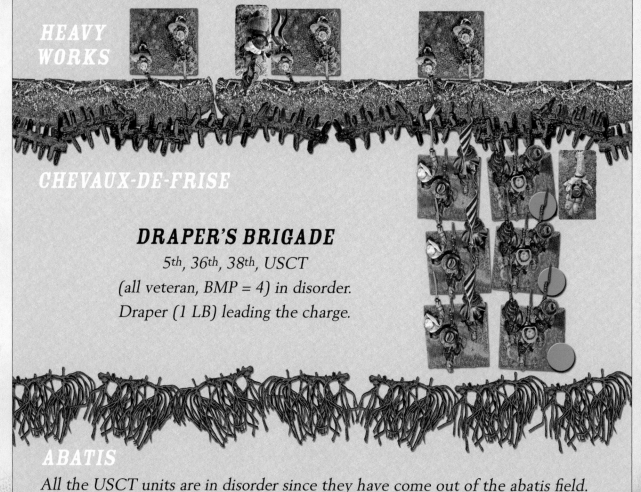

The elite six-figure 4th TX (BMP = 3) is behind heavy works and spread out with one inch between stands. It has a 4 MMP morale benfit for being behind heavy works. Being in works it has no further CMM formation penalties or benefits. Assume that its brigade commander, Lieutenant Colonel Bass (1 LB), is present.

HEAVY WORKS

CHEVAUX-DE-FRISE

DRAPER'S BRIGADE
5th, 36th, 38th, USCT
(all veteran, BMP = 4) in disorder.
Draper (1 LB) leading the charge.

ABATIS

All the USCT units are in disorder since they have come out of the abatis field.

plus the number of figures actually in impact minus the unit's charge or impact MMP.

Example: 4th Texas – in the impact resolution the Final Impact Value (FIV) of the 4th Texas would be calculated as follows: Though the 4th Texas has 6 figures, it only has 2 figures that are actually involved in the impact that can be add to the 2D6 impact die roll from which its charge MMP is subtracted. Its charge MMP starts with its elite BMP of 3, which is improved by a -4 since it is in heavy

works. However, a unit's MMP can never be lower than zero, hence its final charge MMP is zero. This means that its Final Impact Value would be 2D6 +2. So if the 4th Texas rolled a 7, its final total would be a 9.

Example: Draper's Brigade – In the impact resolution, the FIV of the 5th United States Colored Troops would be calculated as follows: The 5th USCT has six figures for a 6 that are actually involved in the impact and that can be added to the 2D6 impact die roll, from which its charge

OPTIONAL REGIMENTAL REDEPLOYMENT: *Just before the impact resolution the stands of the 4th TX could rush to the threatened point so that in the charge impact resolution both sides would have 6 figures in contact...*

...However, while this would certainly help the 4th TX to hold off the charge of Draper's Brigade, any one regiment can only do this once in a turn and it can only do this if it was defending in heavy works which facilitate lateral movements.
And win or lose, the 4th TX is now clumped in front of Draper and the rest of the works are now vacant.

MMP is subtracted. Its charge MMP starts with its veteran BMP of 4, which is worsened by +2 since it is in disorder to a 6. However, it has two regiments in support, which lowers its charge MMP back to a 4, and since it is charging it gets an additional – 1 MMP benefit for a net MMP of 3. However, if the charge was being made with uncapped muskets the 5th USCT would be entitled to an addition -1 MMP benefit. In that case, its final charge MMP would be a 2. This means its Final Impact Value would be 2D6 + 6 – 2. So if the 5th USCT also rolled a 7, its final total would be an 11.

So, in this case, Draper's Brigade, led by the 5th USCT, has won the impact resolution by 2, which means the entire 4th Texas falls back two inches in disorder and loses one figure. Since the charge would have been over a fraise or chevaux-de-frise, the victorious 5th USCT along with the rest of Draper's Brigade can only occupy the space immediately behind the works. Likewise, should another charge come in over the fraise or chevaux-de-frise, those units would also occupy the works rather than being able to pursue the 4th Texas.

Historically, this was how Draper's Brigade broke the Texas line. Simultaneously, Holman's Brigade, with the 22nd USCT in the lead, would peel back the 3rd Arkansas the same way. With their works being penetrated in multiple places and with a second crisis developing along the Varina Road, the Confederates decided to abandon the New Market Heights position.

OPTIONAL REGIMENTAL REDEPLOYMENT

One big advantage of works is that they are usually designed to facilitate rapid lateral movement against the attackers, which are also being slowed by the obstacle field. To show this capability, allow a regiment – right before impact resolution – to concentrate as illustrated. However, allowing a regiment to do this leaves a portion of the works now undefended and should another attack come the position could be compromised.

That was exactly what happened to Hampton's Legion. It concentrated to rebuff the 6th and 7th Connecticut, and then the 3rd New Hampshire and 24th Massachusetts poured over the now vacant flank of the defensive works and began to roll up their position. At that point, the Confederates decided to flee.

Union troops cross the Confederate defences on Marye's Heights, by Adam Hook © Osprey Publishing Ltd. Taken from Campaign 55: Chancellorsville 1863.